What will you do to feel the way you want to feel?

The Desire Map Planner - 2017 Daily (Limited Edition) by Danielle LaPorte
Copyright © 2016 Danielle LaPorte Inc.

All rights reserved, Danielle LaPorte Inc.

ISBN: 978-0-9969052-6-8

Planner graphic design by Laurie Millotte, LaurieMillotte.com
Cover illustration by Marta Spendowska, VeryMarta.com
Astrology by Theresa Reed
Printed and bound in China (We aim to produce everything in North America — hold tight!)

DANIELLELAPORTE.COM

f daniellelaporte.com/facebook
🐦 @daniellelaporte
📌 pinterest.com/daniellelaporte
📷 instagram.com/daniellelaporte

Post pics of your day planner tagged with **#DESIREMAP**
so we can find you and show you some Love!

Go to DESIREMAP.COM/PLANNER for free tools and downloads.

Also by Danielle:
The Desire Map Journal - Volume 1 (Signature Edition)
The Desire Map Journal - Volume 1 (Limited Edition)
The Desire Map Planner - 2017 Weekly (Signature Edition)
The Desire Map Planner - 2017 Weekly (Limited Edition)
The Desire Map Planner - 2017 Daily (Signature Edition)
The Desire Map Daily Planner App
The Desire Map Book + Audio Series
Desire Map Licensing Program
The Fire Starter Sessions Book + Audio Series
#Truthbomb Decks, Volume 1 + Volume 2
The #Truthbomb App
Conversation Starters: A Desire Map App

THE DESIRE MAP

PLANNER

Daily Edition 2017

Danielle
LAPORTE

THE DESIRE MAP

TheDesireMap.com = resources, inspiration and a whole lot of other people on their journey to discover and live their core desired feelings. See you there.

The Desire Map *book...nearly 100k copies sold. 500+* Desire Map *Book Clubs – from Vancouver to Stockholm.* Desire Map *Workshops happen every weekend around the world, facilitated by one of our 800+ licensed* Desire Map Facilitators. *Five language translations.*

One New Year's eve, I had an a-ha about typical goal setting – it was sucking. The a-ha: my "goal" was actually to feel the way I wanted to. So...what if I got clear on how I wanted to feel, and then made things happen that made me feel that way? So simple it was radical.

Desire mapping was born.

Perspective: many of us have our relationship to ambition and goal setting inside out. We're chasing external stuff to do, have, and experience and hope that when we get there, we'll feel awesome – and sometimes we do. But too often, we really don't.

Everything we do is driven by the desire to feel a certain way. Everything. You're not chasing the goal itself, you're chasing the feelings that you hope attaining that goal will give you. So knowing how you want to feel is the most potent clarity you can have. Generating those core desired feelings is the most powerful thing you can do with your life.

Be clear on your core desired feelings, and then all of your goals are a means to create those feelings. It's that simple. And potentially revolutionary. The foundation of a good relationship with intentions and goals is keeping in mind that the primary aim of setting and working toward them is to feel the way you most want to feel. The external things you want to have and experience are in service to your heart and Soul.

Feeling good is the whole point and you get to define exactly what "feeling good" means for you.

It's YOUR life. It's your LIFE.

Hello Love,

If you're using this day planner you're most definitely a soul seeker. Welcome!
This system puts your soul on the agenda – feelings first, then strategy. I'm all
about being productive and making great stuff happen, 100%. I'm also about
fierce Love, wide-awake living, and sweet joy. And truth. So this is a truly
holistic calendar. **All of who you are belongs on these pages.**

You don't need to have gone through my book, *The Desire Map*, to use
this planner. It's universal, so just jump in. Keep it light or go deep. You can
answer the daily Soul Prompts with just one word, or fill up the margins. You
can whisper the mantras or burn some pages. However you go about it, I
hope you'll keep remembering – more deeply every time – how very powerful
you truly are, and that...

AMBITION GOES BETTER WITH A SINCERE AND DARING HEART.

ever true

D xo

PS
We created a *digital* monthly planning booster.
It's called *Goals With Soul*, it's a freebie, and you can download it at
DANIELLELAPORTE.COM/MONTHLY
Now have fun getting all plannery and soulful.

WHAT I WILL DO TO FEEL THE WAY I WANT TO FEEL IN 2017

Knowing how you most want to feel – and setting goals & intentions based on those core desired feelings, is the most **potent form of clarity** you can have.

Desire Mapping is a brilliant New Year ritual, and just as effectual in the Fall, for your birthday, quarterly, and on Full Moons – whenever you need to recalibrate your Soul.

My Core Desired Feelings:

How do you want to feel most of the time?

My major intentions & goals for the year:

Inner attunement + outer attainment. Anchor your core desired feelings to a life design strategy. What are you going to actualize this year – and remember, both goals themselves and the journey to achieve them are a reflection of your core desired feelings.

To fulfill my intentions & goals for 2017, I will:

Deliberate, intentional, heart-centric and in trust. What actions will you take this year to bring your desired feelings and intentions to full life?

2017
overview

Strong preferences = deliberate creation.

JANUARY

WK	M	T	W	T	F	S	S
							1
01	2	3	4	5	6	7	8
02	9	10	11	12	13	14	15
03	16	17	18	19	20	21	22
04	23	24	25	26	27	28	29
05	30	31					

APRIL

WK	M	T	W	T	F	S	S
13						1	2
14	3	4	5	6	7	8	9
15	10	11	12	13	14	15	16
16	17	18	19	20	21	22	23
17	24	25	26	27	28	29	30

JULY

WK	M	T	W	T	F	S	S
26						1	2
27	3	4	5	6	7	8	9
28	10	11	12	13	14	15	16
29	17	18	19	20	21	22	23
30	24	25	26	27	28	29	30
31	31						

OCTOBER

WK	M	T	W	T	F	S	S
39							1
40	2	3	4	5	6	7	8
41	9	10	11	12	13	14	15
42	16	17	18	19	20	21	22
43	23	24	25	26	27	28	29
44	30	31					

FEBRUARY

WK	M	T	W	T	F	S	S
05			1	2	3	4	5
06	6	7	8	9	10	11	12
07	13	14	15	16	17	18	19
08	20	21	22	23	24	25	26
09	27	28					

MARCH

WK	M	T	W	T	F	S	S
09			1	2	3	4	5
10	6	7	8	9	10	11	12
11	13	14	15	16	17	18	19
12	20	21	22	23	24	25	26
13	27	28	29	30	31		

MAY

WK	M	T	W	T	F	S	S
18	1	2	3	4	5	6	7
19	8	9	10	11	12	13	14
20	15	16	17	18	19	20	21
21	22	23	24	25	26	27	28
22	29	30	31				

JUNE

WK	M	T	W	T	F	S	S
22			1	2	3	4	
23	5	6	7	8	9	10	11
24	12	13	14	15	16	17	18
25	19	20	21	22	23	24	25
26	26	27	28	29	30		

AUGUST

WK	M	T	W	T	F	S	S
31		1	2	3	4	5	6
32	7	8	9	10	11	12	13
33	14	15	16	17	18	19	20
34	21	22	23	24	25	26	27
35	28	29	30	31			

SEPTEMBER

WK	M	T	W	T	F	S	S
35					1	2	3
36	4	5	6	7	8	9	10
37	11	12	13	14	15	16	17
38	18	19	20	21	22	23	24
39	25	26	27	28	29	30	

NOVEMBER

WK	M	T	W	T	F	S	S
44			1	2	3	4	5
45	6	7	8	9	10	11	12
46	13	14	15	16	17	18	19
47	20	21	22	23	24	25	26
48	27	28	29	30			

DECEMBER

WK	M	T	W	T	F	S	S
48					1	2	3
49	4	5	6	7	8	9	10
50	11	12	13	14	15	16	17
51	18	19	20	21	22	23	24
52	25	26	27	28	29	30	31

2018
overview

Focus + trust = space for magic to appear.

....
....
....
....
....
....
....
....
....
....
....
....
....
....
....
....
....
....
....

JANUARY

WK	M	T	W	T	F	S	S
1	1	2	3	4	5	6	7
2	8	9	10	11	12	13	14
3	15	16	17	18	19	20	21
4	22	23	24	25	26	27	28
5	29	30	31				

APRIL

WK	M	T	W	T	F	S	S
13							1
14	2	3	4	5	6	7	8
15	9	10	11	12	13	14	15
16	16	17	18	19	20	21	22
17	23	24	25	26	27	28	29
18	30						

JULY

WK	M	T	W	T	F	S	S
26							1
27	2	3	4	5	6	7	8
28	9	10	11	12	13	14	15
29	16	17	18	19	20	21	22
30	23	24	25	26	27	28	29
31	30	31					

OCTOBER

WK	M	T	W	T	F	S	S
40	1	2	3	4	5	6	7
41	8	9	10	11	12	13	14
42	15	16	17	18	19	20	21
43	22	23	24	25	26	27	28
44	29	30	31				

FEBRUARY

WK	M	T	W	T	F	S	S
5				1	2	3	4
6	5	6	7	8	9	10	11
7	12	13	14	15	16	17	18
8	19	20	21	22	23	24	25
9	26	27	28				

MARCH

WK	M	T	W	T	F	S	S
9			1	2	3	4
10	5	6	7	8	9	10	11
11	12	13	14	15	16	17	18
12	19	20	21	22	23	24	25
13	26	27	28	29	30	31	

MAY

WK	M	T	W	T	F	S	S
18		1	2	3	4	5	6
19	7	8	9	10	11	12	13
20	14	15	16	17	18	19	20
21	21	22	23	24	25	26	27
22	28	29	30	31			

JUNE

WK	M	T	W	T	F	S	S
22					1	2	3
23	4	5	6	7	8	9	10
24	11	12	13	14	15	16	17
25	18	19	20	21	22	23	24
26	25	26	27	28	29	30	

AUGUST

WK	M	T	W	T	F	S	S
31			1	2	3	4	5
32	6	7	8	9	10	11	12
33	13	14	15	16	17	18	19
34	20	21	22	23	24	25	26
35	27	28	29	30	31		

SEPTEMBER

WK	M	T	W	T	F	S	S
35						1	2
36	3	4	5	6	7	8	9
37	10	11	12	13	14	15	16
38	17	18	19	20	21	22	23
39	24	25	26	27	28	29	30

NOVEMBER

WK	M	T	W	T	F	S	S
44			1	2	3	4
45	5	6	7	8	9	10	11
46	12	13	14	15	16	17	18
47	19	20	21	22	23	24	25
48	26	27	28	29	30		

DECEMBER

WK	M	T	W	T	F	S	S
48						1	2
49	3	4	5	6	7	8	9
50	10	11	12	13	14	15	16
51	17	18	19	20	21	22	23
52	24	25	26	27	28	29	30
53	31						

JANUARY

2017

adventurous

alive

aliveness

dynamic

energy

energetic

energized

enthusiastic

excited

exuberance

healing

health

healthy

robust

vital

vitality

vitalized

MONDAY	TUESDAY	WEDNESDAY
2	3	4
WEEK 1		
9	10	11
WEEK 2		
Martin Luther King, Jr. Day (US) 16	17	18
WEEK 3		
23	24	25
WEEK 4		
30	31	
WEEK 5		

THURSDAY	FRIDAY	SATURDAY	SUNDAY
			New Year's Day **Hanukkah 2016 ends (evening)** 1
5	6	7	Mercury turns direct 8
O Full Moon 12	13	14	15
Sun enters Aquarius 19	20	21	22
Australia Day 26	● New Moon 27	28	29

JANUARY 2017 MONTHLY CHECK-IN

My Core Desired Feelings:

Feelings inform your wellness, your creations, your wisdom. Tune in to the predominant and new feelings that are running through you these days.

My major intentions & goals for the year:

Revisit your vision. When your core desired feelings lead the way, both your goals and how you go after them become more satisfying. How are your goals a reflection of how you most want to feel?

To generate my CDFs through my intentions & goals, I will:

What will it take to fulfill your vision for the year? Evaluate, affirm, or adjust your to-dos and intentions according to what you think will generate your core desired feelings along the way.

IMPACTFUL

IDEAS. DESIRES. WISDOM. ... leave room for magic & meandering

NURTURING

New Year's Day | Hanukkah 2016 ends (evening)

WHAT I WILL DO TO FEEL THE WAY I WANT TO FEEL

TO-DO ... your desires are sacred

....

....

....

....

ENVISION ... my words for the New Year are:

Make space in your life for the inevitable arrival of what you want.

TETHERED

MY CORE DESIRED FEELINGS

WHAT I WILL DO TO FEEL
THE WAY I WANT TO FEEL

SOUL PROMPT ... what is your greatest desire?

SCHEDULE ... simplicity is freedom

:

:

:

:

:

:

:

:

:

:

:

:

:

3 THINGS ... get this done and the rest is a bonus

TO-DO ... keep your soul on the agenda

STOP DOING ... *No* makes way for *Yes*

WANT TO CHANGE ... claim it. Tame it.

GRATITUDE ... specificity intensifies gratitude

RESILIENT

Your FEELINGS are THE SIGN you've been looking for.

MY CORE DESIRED FEELINGS

WHAT I WILL DO TO FEEL THE WAY I WANT TO FEEL

SOUL PROMPT ... how did you feel when you woke up today?

SCHEDULE ... reframe "obligations" into "choices"

:
:
:
:
:
:
:
:
:
:
:
:
:
:

3 THINGS ... that are moving your life forward

TO-DO ... prioritize pleasure

STOP DOING ... work for Love

WANT TO CHANGE ... the solution will come

GRATITUDE ... note WHY you're grateful

The universe will configure around your best efforts.

LAVISH

MY CORE DESIRED FEELINGS

WHAT I WILL DO TO FEEL
THE WAY I WANT TO FEEL

SOUL PROMPT ... how do you want to feel when you go to bed tonight?

SCHEDULE ... does it light you up?

:
:
:
:
:
:
:
:
:
:
:
:
:
:

3 THINGS ... that are doable today

TO-DO ... less striving, more living

STOP DOING ... don't take any crap

WANT TO CHANGE ... clarity is power

GRATITUDE ... puts everything into perspective

fierce faith

PURE

WHAT I WILL DO TO FEEL THE WAY I WANT TO FEEL

SOUL PROMPT ... today, my heart feels

SCHEDULE ... respect yourself

- :
- :
- :
- :
- :
- :
- :
- :
- :
- :
- :
- :
- :

3 THINGS ... that matter most

TO-DO ... the WHOLE point is to feel good

STOP DOING ... does it feel light or heavy?

WANT TO CHANGE ... why should it be different?

GRATITUDE ... challenges are teachers

TOUCHED

It helps to be clear on exactly what you're leaving behind.

MY CORE DESIRED FEELINGS

WHAT I WILL DO TO FEEL
THE WAY I WANT TO FEEL

SOUL PROMPT ... I want to revolutionize

SCHEDULE ... joy expands time

- :
- :
- :
- :
- :
- :
- :
- :
- :
- :
- :
- :
- :
- :

3 THINGS ... because focus creates momentum

TO-DO ... it's your life. YOUR life. Your LIFE.

STOP DOING ... freedom is your birthright

WANT TO CHANGE ... naming it is liberating

GRATITUDE ... expands your consciousness

COZY

Trust helps the insights to surface.

WHAT I WILL DO TO FEEL
THE WAY I WANT TO FEEL

TO-DO ... make choices that liberate you

....
....
....
....
....

REFLECT ... speak up

TO-DO ... your desires are sacred

....
....
....
....
....

ENVISION ... your soul is rooting for you

SWEET

Lack of passion is fatal.

MY CORE DESIRED FEELINGS

WHAT I WILL DO TO FEEL
THE WAY I WANT TO FEEL

SOUL PROMPT ... what do you wish people knew about you?

SCHEDULE ... simplicity is freedom

: ....
: ....
: ....
: ....
: ....
: ....
: ....
: ....
: ....
: ....
: ....
: ....
: ....
: ....

3 THINGS ... get this done and the rest is a bonus

TO-DO ... keep your soul on the agenda

STOP DOING ... *No* makes way for *Yes*

WANT TO CHANGE ... claim it. Tame it.

GRATITUDE ... specificity intensifies gratitude

INSPIRED

Notice all the prayers in your life that have been answered.

MY CORE DESIRED FEELINGS

WHAT I WILL DO TO FEEL
THE WAY I WANT TO FEEL

SOUL PROMPT ... I've worked hard to

SCHEDULE ... reframe "obligations" into "choices"

3 THINGS ... that are moving your life forward

TO-DO ... prioritize pleasure

STOP DOING ... work for Love

WANT TO CHANGE ... the solution will come

GRATITUDE ... note WHY you're grateful

UNLIMITED

A feeling is stronger than a thought.

MY CORE DESIRED FEELINGS

WHAT I WILL DO TO FEEL
THE WAY I WANT TO FEEL

SOUL PROMPT ... if you didn't do work today, what would you do instead?

SCHEDULE ... does it light you up?

3 THINGS ... that are doable today

TO-DO ... less striving, more living

STOP DOING ... don't take any crap

WANT TO CHANGE ... clarity is power

GRATITUDE ... puts everything into perspective

DIVINELY GUIDED

You can be scared, and really ready.

MY CORE DESIRED FEELINGS

WHAT I WILL DO TO FEEL
THE WAY I WANT TO FEEL

SOUL PROMPT ... today, my heart feels

SCHEDULE ... respect yourself

3 THINGS ... that matter most

TO-DO ... the WHOLE point is to feel good

STOP DOING ... does it feel light or heavy?

WANT TO CHANGE ... why should it be different?

GRATITUDE ... challenges are teachers

TRUE

You can't really know your power until you exercise it.

MY CORE DESIRED FEELINGS

WHAT I WILL DO TO FEEL
THE WAY I WANT TO FEEL

SOUL PROMPT ... one word to describe my style

SCHEDULE ... joy expands time

:
:
:
:
:
:
:
:
:
:
:
:
:
:

3 THINGS ... because focus creates momentum

TO-DO ... it's your life. YOUR life. Your LIFE.

STOP DOING ... freedom is your birthright

WANT TO CHANGE ... naming it is liberating

GRATITUDE ... expands your consciousness

It's all about the why.

BUOYANT

WHAT I WILL DO TO FEEL
THE WAY I WANT TO FEEL

TO-DO ... make choices that liberate you

· ·

· ·

· ·

· ·

· ·

REFLECT ... enthusiasm saves lives

TO-DO ... your desires are sacred

· ·

· ·

· ·

· ·

ENVISION ... I'm devoted to

GODDESS

Your soul is the Love of all Loves.

Martin Luther King, Jr. Day (US)

MY CORE DESIRED FEELINGS

WHAT COLLECT
THE ABOUT WC

SOUL PROMPT ... I give myself permission to

SCHEDULE ... simplicity is freedom

:

:

:

:

:

:

:

:

:

:

:

:

:

:

3 THINGS ... get this done and the rest is a bonus

TO-DO ... keep your soul on the agenda

STOP DOING ... *No makes way for Yes*

WANT TO CHANGE ... claim it. Tame it.

GRATITUDE ... specificity intensifies gratitude

You become what you worship.

CLEAR

MY CORE DESIRED FEELINGS

WHAT I WILL DO TO FEEL
THE WAY I WANT TO FEEL

SOUL PROMPT ... in terms of my livelihood, my greatest desire is

SCHEDULE ... reframe "obligations" into "choices"

3 THINGS ... that are moving your life forward

TO-DO ... prioritize pleasure

STOP DOING ... work for Love

WANT TO CHANGE ... the solution will come

GRATITUDE ... note WHY you're grateful

ENGAGED

You don't need to know the answer before you begin.

MY CORE DESIRED FEELINGS

WHAT
THE

SOUL PROMPT ... what's in your heart right in this moment?

SCHEDULE ... does it light you up?

:

:

:

:

:

:

:

:

:

:

:

:

:

:

3 THINGS ... that are doable today

TO-DO ... less striving, more living

STOP DOING ... don't take any crap

WANT TO CHANGE ... clarity is power

GRATITUDE ... puts everything into perspective

We heal together.

ENRAPTURED

MY CORE DESIRED FEELINGS

WHAT I WILL DO TO FEEL
THE WAY I WANT TO FEEL

SOUL PROMPT ... today, my heart feels

SCHEDULE ... respect yourself

3 THINGS ... that matter most

TO-DO ... the WHOLE point is to feel good

STOP DOING ... does it feel light or heavy?

WANT TO CHANGE ... why should it be different?

GRATITUDE ... challenges are teachers

AUDACIOUS

Meet the universe half way.

MY CORE DESIRED FEELINGS

SOUL PROMPT ... what things in your life make you feel like the opposite of yourself?

SCHEDULE ... joy expands time

  :

  :

  :

  :

  :

  :

  :

  :

  :

  :

  :

  :

  :

  :

3 THINGS ... because focus creates momentum

TO-DO ... it's your life. YOUR life. Your LIFE.

STOP DOING ... freedom is your birthright

WANT TO CHANGE ... naming it is liberating

GRATITUDE ... expands your consciousness

If "liberation" feels like a chore, it isn't really liberation, is it?

FORTUNATE

WHAT I WILL DO TO FEEL
THE WAY I WANT TO FEEL

TO-DO ... make choices that liberate you

TO-DO ... your desires are sacred

REFLECT ... rest

ENVISION ... don't hold back

AFLAME

Conjure up your worst-case scenario. It will liberate you.

WHAT I BELIEVE
THE REASON

SOUL PROMPT ... other than time or money, I want more

SCHEDULE ... simplicity is freedom

:
:
:
:
:
:
:
:
:
:
:
:
:
:

3 THINGS ... get this done and the rest is a bonus

TO-DO ... keep your soul on the agenda

STOP DOING ... *No makes way for Yes*

WANT TO CHANGE ... claim it. Tame it.

GRATITUDE ... specificity intensifies gratitude

Let the miracle take you over.

HEROIC

MY CORE DESIRED FEELINGS

I WILL DO TO FEEL
I WANT TO FEEL

SOUL PROMPT ... what can we count on you for?

SCHEDULE ... reframe "obligations" into "choices"

:
:
:
:
:
:
:
:
:
:
:
:
:
:

3 THINGS ... that are moving your life forward

TO-DO ... prioritize pleasure

STOP DOING ... work for Love

WANT TO CHANGE ... the solution will come

GRATITUDE ... note WHY you're grateful

CHERISHED

Make choices that liberate you.

MY CORE DESIRED FEELINGS

SOUL PROMPT ... how do you want to feel when you get dressed in the morning?

SCHEDULE ... does it light you up?

:

:

:

:

:

:

:

:

:

:

:

:

:

:

3 THINGS ... that are doable today

TO-DO ... less striving, more living

STOP DOING ... don't take any crap

WANT TO CHANGE ... clarity is power

GRATITUDE ... puts everything into perspective

LIGHTHEARTED

Feel your way.

MY CORE DESIRED FEELINGS

WHAT I WILL DO TO FEEL
THE WAY I WANT TO FEEL

SOUL PROMPT ... today, my heart feels

SCHEDULE ... respect yourself

:
:
:
:
:
:
:
:
:
:
:
:
:
:

3 THINGS ... that matter most

TO-DO ... the WHOLE point is to feel good

STOP DOING ... does it feel light or heavy?

WANT TO CHANGE ... why should it be different?

GRATITUDE ... challenges are teachers

ATTENTIVE

Focus + trust = space for magic to appear.

WHAT I WILL DO TO FEEL
THE WAY I WANT TO FEEL

SOUL PROMPT ... it would be a miracle if

SCHEDULE ... joy expands time

:

:

:

:

:

:

:

:

:

:

:

:

:

:

3 THINGS ... because focus creates momentum

TO-DO ... it's your life. YOUR life. Your LIFE.

STOP DOING ... freedom is your birthright

WANT TO CHANGE ... naming it is liberating

GRATITUDE ... expands your consciousness

Forgetting who you are is only a temporary situation.

JOY

TO-DO ... make choices that liberate you   **TO-DO** ... your desires are sacred

REFLECT ... this week I learned   **ENVISION** ... what do you *really* want to happen?

FREE-SPIRITED

Everything is a divine message because life is always calling you.

WHAT
THE

SOUL PROMPT ... what would you Love more of in your life?

SCHEDULE ... simplicity is freedom

3 THINGS... get this done and the rest is a bonus

:

:

:

: **TO-DO** ... keep your soul on the agenda

:

:

:

:

:

:

: **STOP DOING** ... *No makes way for Yes*

:

:

:

WANT TO CHANGE ... claim it. Tame it.

GRATITUDE ... specificity intensifies gratitude

There's always more to let go of.

ORGANIC

MY CORE DESIRED FEELINGS

WHAT I WILL DO TO FEEL
THE WAY I WANT TO FEEL

SOUL PROMPT ... what's your favourite way to show Love?

SCHEDULE ... reframe "obligations" into "choices"

:
:
:
:
:
:
:
:
:
:
:
:
:

3 THINGS ... that are moving your life forward

TO-DO ... prioritize pleasure

STOP DOING ... work for Love

WANT TO CHANGE ... the solution will come

GRATITUDE ... note WHY you're grateful

GIVING

Your voice is your liberation.

IDEAS. DESIRES. WISDOM. ... when you honour your time, you honour you

What makes you feel real?

PATIENT

FEBRUARY

2017

balance

balanced

calm

calming

centred

ease

easeful

equilibrium

harmony

harmonious

heavenly

peace

peaceful

serene

serenity

simplicity

tranquility

FEBRUARY

MONDAY	TUESDAY	WEDNESDAY
		Imbolc 1
WEEK 5		
6	7	8
WEEK 6		
13	**Valentine's Day** 14	15
WEEK 7		
Presidents Day (US) 20	21	22
WEEK 8		
27	**Shrove Tuesday/ Mardi Gras** 28	
WEEK 9		

THURSDAY	FRIDAY	SATURDAY	SUNDAY
Groundhog Day 2	3	4	5
9	O Full Moon Lunar Eclipse 10	11	12
16	17	Sun enters Pisces 18	19
23	24	25	● New Moon Solar Eclipse 26

FEBRUARY

FEBRUARY 2017 MONTHLY CHECK-IN

My Core Desired Feelings:

Feelings inform your wellness, your creations, your wisdom. Tune in to the predominant and new feelings that are running through you these days.

My major intentions & goals for the year:

Revisit your vision. When your core desired feelings lead the way, both your goals and how you go after them become more satisfying. How are your goals a reflection of how you most want to feel?

To generate my CDFs through my intentions & goals, I will:

What will it take to fulfill your vision for the year? Evaluate, affirm, or adjust your to-dos and intentions according to what you think will generate your core desired feelings along the way.

ENRICHED

ORIGINAL

MY CORE DESIRED FEELINGS

WHAT I WILL DO TO FEEL THE WAY I WANT TO FEEL

SOUL PROMPT ... what are the small things that you Love to pay attention to?

SCHEDULE ... does it light you up?

:
:
:
:
:
:
:
:
:
:
:
:
:
:

3 THINGS ... that are doable today

TO-DO ... less striving, more living

STOP DOING ... don't take any crap

WANT TO CHANGE ... clarity is power

GRATITUDE ... puts everything into perspective

EMBODIED

Dream like an eagle. Plan like a mouse.

THURSDAY February 2 | 2017
Groundhog Day

MY CORE DESIRED FEELINGS

SOUL PROMPT ... where do you feel the pull to rebel?

SCHEDULE ... respect yourself

:

:

:

:

:

:

:

:

:

:

:

:

:

:

3 THINGS ... that matter most

TO-DO ... the WHOLE point is to feel good

STOP DOING ... does it feel light or heavy?

WANT TO CHANGE ... why should it be different?

GRATITUDE ... challenges are teachers

According to who? According to You.

SHAKTI

MY CORE DESIRED FEELINGS

WHAT I WILL DO TO FEEL
THE WAY I WANT TO FEEL

SOUL PROMPT ... today, my heart feels

SCHEDULE ... joy expands time

:
:
:
:
:
:
:
:
:
:
:
:
:
:

3 THINGS ... because focus creates momentum

TO-DO ... it's your life. YOUR life. Your LIFE.

STOP DOING ... freedom is your birthright

WANT TO CHANGE ... naming it is liberating

GRATITUDE ... expands your consciousness

RECEPTIVE

Stream your consciousness.

TO-DO ... make choices that liberate you

TO-DO ... your desires are sacred

REFLECT ... what's true for you?

ENVISION ... let it be easy

Feel the original Yes that your soul said to being here.

THRIVING

MY CORE DESIRED FEELINGS

SOUL PROMPT ... what reminds you of who you truly are?

SCHEDULE ... simplicity is freedom

:
:
:
:
:
:
:
:
:
:
:
:
:
:

WANT TO CHANGE ... claim it. Tame it.

3 THINGS ... get this done and the rest is a bonus

TO-DO ... keep your soul on the agenda

STOP DOING ... *No* makes way for *Yes*

GRATITUDE ... specificity intensifies gratitude

PEACEFUL

Get clear on why you're chasing what you're chasing.

MY CORE DESIRED FEELINGS

SOUL PROMPT ... how do you want to feel when you look in the mirror?

SCHEDULE ... reframe "obligations" into "choices"

:

:

:

:

:

:

:

:

:

:

:

:

:

:

3 THINGS ... that are moving your life forward

TO-DO ... prioritize pleasure

STOP DOING ... work for Love

WANT TO CHANGE ... the solution will come

GRATITUDE ... note WHY you're grateful

Love transcends policy and history.

SPIRITED

MY CORE DESIRED FEELINGS

WHAT I WILL DO TO FEEL
THE WAY I WANT TO FEEL

SOUL PROMPT ... what I do most naturally is

SCHEDULE ... does it light you up?

3 THINGS ... that are doable today

:

:

:

:

TO-DO ... less striving, more living

:

:

:

:

:

:

:

STOP DOING ... don't take any crap

:

:

:

:

WANT TO CHANGE ... clarity is power

GRATITUDE ... puts everything into perspective

ON FIRE

Small acts of freedom will really change your life.

MY CORE DESIRED FEELINGS

WHAT
THE

SOUL PROMPT ... I'm avoiding

SCHEDULE ... respect yourself

:

:

:

:

:

:

:

:

:

:

:

:

:

:

3 THINGS ... that matter most

TO-DO ... the WHOLE point is to feel good

STOP DOING ... does it feel light or heavy?

WANT TO CHANGE ... why should it be different?

GRATITUDE ... challenges are teachers

VIBRANT

Desire sees possibility everywhere.

MY CORE DESIRED FEELINGS

WHAT I WILL DO TO FEEL
THE WAY I WANT TO FEEL

SOUL PROMPT ... today, my heart feels

SCHEDULE ... joy expands time

:
:
:
:
:
:
:
:
:
:
:
:
:

3 THINGS ... because focus creates momentum

TO-DO ... it's your life. YOUR life. Your LIFE.

STOP DOING ... freedom is your birthright

WANT TO CHANGE ... naming it is liberating

GRATITUDE ... expands your consciousness

SERENE

Passion over perfection.

TO-DO ... make choices that liberate you

TO-DO ... your desires are sacred

REFLECT ... speak up

ENVISION ... your soul is rooting for you

Get your needs met.

FLUID

MY CORE DESIRED FEELINGS

WHAT I WILL DO TO FEEL
THE WAY I WANT TO FEEL

SOUL PROMPT ... how do you greet friends?

SCHEDULE ... simplicity is freedom

:
:
:
:
:
:
:
:
:
:
:
:
:
:

3 THINGS ... get this done and the rest is a bonus

TO-DO ... keep your soul on the agenda

STOP DOING ... *No* makes way for *Yes*

WANT TO CHANGE ... claim it. Tame it.

GRATITUDE ... specificity intensifies gratitude

UNDERSTOOD

Move toward pleasure, rather than away from pain.

TUESDAY February 14 | 2017

Valentine's Day

WH
THE

MY CORE DESIRED FEELINGS

SOUL PROMPT ... what do you hope is true?

SCHEDULE ... reframe "obligations" into "choices"

:
:
:
:
:
:
:
:
:
:
:
:
:
:

3 THINGS ... that are moving your life forward

TO-DO ... prioritize pleasure

STOP DOING ... work for Love

WANT TO CHANGE ... the solution will come

GRATITUDE ... note WHY you're grateful

love rewards the brave

GENEROUS

SOUL PROMPT ... what are 3 things you would do on your ideal day?

SCHEDULE ... does it light you up?

3 THINGS ... that are doable today

:
:
:
:
:
:
:
:
:
:
:
:
:
:

TO-DO ... less striving, more living

STOP DOING.. don't take any crap

WANT TO CHANGE ... clarity is power

GRATITUDE ... puts everything into perspective

FREE

True intimacy trumps technique.

MY CORE DESIRED FEELINGS

SOUL PROMPT ... what can you do to feel more connected to the person you Love the most?

SCHEDULE ... respect yourself

:
:
:
:
:
:
:
:
:
:
:
:
:
:

3 THINGS ... that matter most

TO-DO ... the WHOLE point is to feel good

STOP DOING ... does it feel light or heavy?

WANT TO CHANGE ... why should it be different?

GRATITUDE ... challenges are teachers

INDULGENT

Eat light.

WHAT I WILL DO TO FEEL
THE WAY I WANT TO FEEL

SOUL PROMPT ... today, my heart feels

SCHEDULE ... joy expands time

:
:
:
:
:
:
:
:
:
:
:
:
:
:

3 THINGS ... because focus creates momentum

TO-DO ... it's your life. YOUR life. Your LIFE.

STOP DOING ... freedom is your birthright

WANT TO CHANGE ... naming it is liberating

GRATITUDE ... expands your consciousness

EXPANSIVE

Going without, and holding out, is better than selling out.

WHAT
THE

TO-DO ... make choices that liberate you

TO-DO ... your desires are sacred

REFLECT ... enthusiasm saves lives

ENVISION ... I'm devoted to

You can't plant misery seeds today and expect to get a juicy crop next season.

HEALTHY

MY CORE DESIRED FEELINGS

WHAT I WILL DO TO FEEL
THE WAY I WANT TO FEEL

SOUL PROMPT ... what would make you feel really Loved right now?

SCHEDULE ... simplicity is freedom

:
:
:
:
:
:
:
:
:
:
:
:
:
:
:

WANT TO CHANGE ... claim it. Tame it.

3 THINGS ... get this done and the rest is a bonus

TO-DO ... keep your soul on the agenda

STOP DOING ... *No* makes way for *Yes*

GRATITUDE ... specificity intensifies gratitude

COMPLETE

Surrender isn't about being passive. It's about being open.

MY CORE DESIRED FEELINGS

SOUL PROMPT ... what risk is tugging at your soul?

SCHEDULE ... reframe "obligations" into "choices"

:

:

:

:

:

:

:

:

:

:

:

:

:

:

WANT TO CHANGE ... the solution will come

3 THINGS ... that are moving your life forward

TO-DO ... prioritize pleasure

STOP DOING ... work for Love

GRATITUDE ... note WHY you're grateful

INSIGHTFUL

Want more. (Inner peace, greater clarity, outer beauty, awesome stuff – want anything you want.)

WHAT I WILL DO TO FEEL
THE WAY I WANT TO FEEL

SOUL PROMPT ... what needs to go on your "stop doing" list?

SCHEDULE ... does it light you up?

3 THINGS ... that are doable today

:
:
:
:
:
:
:
:
:
:
:
:
:
:

TO-DO ... less striving, more living

STOP DOING ... don't take any crap

WANT TO CHANGE ... clarity is power

GRATITUDE ... puts everything into perspective

ARTISTIC

MY CORE DESIRED FEELINGS

WHAT
THE

SOUL PROMPT ... one beautiful idea

SCHEDULE ... respect yourself

:
:
:
:
:
:
:
:
:
:
:
:
:
:

3 THINGS ... that matter most

TO-DO ... the WHOLE point is to feel good

STOP DOING ... does it feel light or heavy?

WANT TO CHANGE ... why should it be different?

GRATITUDE ... challenges are teachers

The surest way to simplify your life is to focus on what matters most.

DELIBERATE

MY CORE DESIRED FEELINGS

I WILL DO TO FEEL
THE WAY I WANT TO FEEL

SOUL PROMPT ... today, my heart feels

SCHEDULE ... joy expands time

:
:
:
:
:
:
:
:
:
:
:
:
:
:

WANT TO CHANGE ... naming it is liberating

3 THINGS ... because focus creates momentum

TO-DO ... it's your life. YOUR life. Your LIFE.

STOP DOING ... freedom is your birthright

GRATITUDE ... expands your consciousness

ADORED

Inner attunement over outer attainment.

SATURDAY February 25 | 2017

SUNDAY February 26 | 2017
● New Moon | Solar Eclipse

TO-DO ... make choices that liberate you

TO-DO ... your desires are sacred

REFLECT ... rest

ENVISION ... don't hold back

AUTHENTIC

Have an idea, or two or three, about how to get more. Act on that idea over and over again.

MY CORE DESIRED FEELINGS

WHAT I WILL DO TO FEEL
THE WAY I WANT TO FEEL

SOUL PROMPT ... five beautiful things I can see right now

SCHEDULE ... simplicity is freedom

3 THINGS ... get this done and the rest is a bonus

TO-DO ... keep your soul on the agenda

STOP DOING ... *No* makes way for *Yes*

WANT TO CHANGE ... claim it. Tame it.

GRATITUDE ... specificity intensifies gratitude

CHOSEN

Write the letter. (You don't have to send it.) Just write it out.

WHAT WILL I DO WITH
THE MADNESS

SOUL PROMPT ... what do you care about most deeply?

SCHEDULE ... reframe "obligations" into "choices"

- :
- :
- :
- :
- :
- :
- :
- :
- :
- :
- :
- :
- :
- :

3 THINGS ... that are moving your life forward

TO-DO ... prioritize pleasure

STOP DOING ... work for Love

WANT TO CHANGE ... the solution will come

GRATITUDE ... note WHY you're grateful

Renew your vows.

BRAVE

MARCH
2017

audacious

bold

brave

bravery

confidence

confident

courage

courageous

daring

embolden

empowered

enterprising

lion-hearted

strength

strong

MONDAY	TUESDAY	WEDNESDAY
		1
WEEK 9		
6	7	8
WEEK 10		
Commonwealth Day (CAN, AUS, UK) 13	14	15
WEEK 11		
Spring Equinox/ Ostara 20 Sun enters Aries	**Harmony Day (AUS)** 21	22
WEEK 12		
● New Moon 27	28	29
WEEK 13		

THURSDAY	FRIDAY	SATURDAY	SUNDAY
2	3	4	5
9	10	11 **Purim begins (evening)**	12 **Purim ends (evening)** **Daylight saving time starts** ○ Full Moon
16	17 **St. Patrick's Day**	18	19
23	24	25	26
30	31		

MARCH 2017 MONTHLY CHECK-IN

My Core Desired Feelings:

Feelings inform your wellness, your creations, your wisdom. Tune in to the predominant and new feelings that are running through you these days.

My major intentions & goals for the year:

Revisit your vision. When your core desired feelings lead the way, both your goals and how you go after them become more satisfying. How are your goals a reflection of how you most want to feel?

To generate my CDFs through my intentions & goals, I will:

What will it take to fulfill your vision for the year? Evaluate, affirm, or adjust your to-dos and intentions according to what you think will generate your core desired feelings along the way.

INTRIGUING

IDEAS. DESIRES. WISDOM. ... take up space

ARTFUL

MY CORE DESIRED FEELINGS

SOUL PROMPT ... when do you get that "called to the principal's office" feeling of dread?

SCHEDULE ... does it light you up?

- :
- :
- :
- :
- :
- :
- :
- :
- :
- :
- :
- :
- :
- :

3 THINGS ... that are doable today

TO-DO ... less striving, more living

STOP DOING ... don't take any crap

WANT TO CHANGE ... clarity is power

GRATITUDE ... puts everything into perspective

HOLY

This is not a test.

MY CORE DESIRED FEELINGS

SOUL PROMPT ... today, my heart feels

SCHEDULE ... respect yourself

:

:

:

:

:

:

:

:

:

:

:

:

:

:

3 THINGS ... that matter most

TO-DO ... the WHOLE point is to feel good

STOP DOING ... does it feel light or heavy?

WANT TO CHANGE ... why should it be different?

GRATITUDE ... challenges are teachers

EXCITED

Empathy is the great healer.

WHAT I WILL DO TO FEEL
THE WAY I WANT TO FEEL

SOUL PROMPT ... two beautiful experiences

SCHEDULE ... joy expands time

3 THINGS ... because focus creates momentum

TO-DO ... it's your life. YOUR life. Your LIFE.

STOP DOING ... freedom is your birthright

WANT TO CHANGE ... naming it is liberating

GRATITUDE ... expands your consciousness

LOVELY

Conformity sucks.

WHAT
THE WA

TO-DO ... make choices that liberate you

TO-DO ... your desires are sacred

REFLECT ... this week I learned

ENVISION ... what do you *really* want to happen?

The only thing that you really have control over is your feelings.

BLOSSOMING

MY CORE DESIRED FEELINGS

WILL DO TO FEEL

WANT TO FEEL

SOUL PROMPT ... I need to do less

SCHEDULE ... simplicity is freedom

3 THINGS ... get this done and the rest is a bonus

:
:
:
:

TO-DO ... keep your soul on the agenda

:
:
:
:
:
:

STOP DOING ... *No* makes way for *Yes*

:
:
:

WANT TO CHANGE ... claim it. Tame it.

GRATITUDE ... specificity intensifies gratitude

PLAYFUL

You are healing.

WHAT
THE

SOUL PROMPT ... three words that come to mind when you read the word "time"

SCHEDULE ... reframe "obligations" into "choices"

:

:

:

:

:

:

:

:

:

:

:

:

:

:

3 THINGS ... that are moving your life forward

TO-DO ... prioritize pleasure

STOP DOING ... work for Love

WANT TO CHANGE ... the solution will come

GRATITUDE ... note WHY you're grateful

Nothing changes without you.

EUPHORIC

WHAT I WILL DO TO FEEL
THE WAY I WANT TO FEEL

SOUL PROMPT ... what are you praying for right now?

SCHEDULE ... does it light you up?

3 THINGS ... that are doable today

:
:
:
:
:

TO-DO ... less striving, more living

:
:
:
:
:

STOP DOING ... don't take any crap

:
:
:
:

WANT TO CHANGE ... clarity is power

GRATITUDE ... puts everything into perspective

RAPTUROUS

Start where it's easy.

SOUL PROMPT ... today, my heart feels

SCHEDULE ... respect yourself

:

:

:

:

:

:

:

:

:

:

:

:

:

:

3 THINGS ... that matter most

TO-DO ... the WHOLE point is to feel good

STOP DOING ... does it feel light or heavy?

WANT TO CHANGE ... why should it be different?

GRATITUDE ... challenges are teachers

Say what your Soul needs to say.

GUIDED

WHAT I WILL DO TO FEEL
THE WAY I WANT TO FEEL

SOUL PROMPT ... my three favourite possessions

SCHEDULE ... joy expands time

    ⋮

    ⋮

    ⋮

    ⋮

    ⋮

    ⋮

    ⋮

    ⋮

    ⋮

    ⋮

    ⋮

    ⋮

    ⋮

3 THINGS ... because focus creates momentum

TO-DO ... it's your life. YOUR life. Your LIFE.

STOP DOING ... freedom is your birthright

WANT TO CHANGE ... naming it is liberating

GRATITUDE ... expands your consciousness

NOURISHED

It won't change until you admit to the pain.

SATURDAY March 11 | 2017

Purim begins (evening)

WHAT
THE

TO-DO ... make choices that liberate you

REFLECT ... what's true for you?

SUNDAY March 12 | 2017

Purim ends (evening) | Daylight saving time starts
○ Full Moon

TO-DO ... your desires are sacred

ENVISION ... let it be easy

Notice when your dream has come true.

SULTRY

MY CORE DESIRED FEELINGS

WHAT I WILL DO TO FEEL
THE WAY I WANT TO FEEL

SOUL PROMPT ... I feel close to life when

SCHEDULE ... simplicity is freedom

:

:

:

:

:

:

:

:

:

:

:

:

:

3 THINGS ... get this done and the rest is a bonus

TO-DO ... keep your soul on the agenda

STOP DOING ... *No* makes way for *Yes*

WANT TO CHANGE ... claim it. Tame it.

GRATITUDE ... specificity intensifies gratitude

SURRENDERED

All light all the time.

SOUL PROMPT ... my creativity

SCHEDULE ... reframe "obligations" into "choices"

:

:

:

:

:

:

:

:

:

:

:

:

:

:

3 THINGS ... that are moving your life forward

TO-DO ... prioritize pleasure

STOP DOING ... work for Love

WANT TO CHANGE ... the solution will come

GRATITUDE ... note WHY you're grateful

Destruction before creation.

TENACIOUS

MY CORE DESIRED FEELINGS

WHAT I WILL DO TO FEEL
THE WAY I WANT TO FEEL

SOUL PROMPT ... what in your life are you forcing?

SCHEDULE ... does it light you up?

3 THINGS ... that are doable today

TO-DO ... less striving, more living

STOP DOING ... don't take any crap

WANT TO CHANGE ... clarity is power

GRATITUDE ... puts everything into perspective

UNWAVERING

Tell people what you're doing that's working.

MY CORE DESIRED FEELINGS

W H A T
T H E

SOUL PROMPT ... today, my heart feels

SCHEDULE ... respect yourself

  :

  :

  :

  :

  :

  :

  :

  :

  :

  :

  :

  :

  :

  :

3 THINGS ... that matter most

TO-DO ... the WHOLE point is to feel good

STOP DOING ... does it feel light or heavy?

WANT TO CHANGE ... why should it be different?

GRATITUDE ... challenges are teachers

Keep slaying what's not working. ("Thank you and goodbye, I'm focused on incredible.")

OPTIMISTIC

WHAT I WILL DO TO FEEL
THE WAY I WANT TO FEEL

SOUL PROMPT ... what do you want more than anything?

SCHEDULE ... joy expands time

:

:

:

:

:

:

:

:

:

:

:

:

:

:

3 THINGS ... because focus creates momentum

TO-DO ... it's your life. YOUR life. Your LIFE.

STOP DOING ... freedom is your birthright

WANT TO CHANGE ... naming it is liberating

GRATITUDE ... expands your consciousness

SEXY

Self-deception is part of self-discovery.

TO-DO ... make choices that liberate you

TO-DO ... your desires are sacred

REFLECT ... speak up

ENVISION ... your soul is rooting for you

Enthusiasm is a heightened state of consciousness.

PASSIONATE

MY CORE DESIRED FEELINGS

WHAT I WILL DO TO FEEL
THE WAY I WANT TO FEEL

SOUL PROMPT ... I honour

SCHEDULE ... simplicity is freedom

:
:
:
:
:
:
:
:
:
:
:
:
:
:

3 THINGS ... get this done and the rest is a bonus

TO-DO ... keep your soul on the agenda

STOP DOING ... *No* makes way for *Yes*

WANT TO CHANGE ... claim it. Tame it.

GRATITUDE ... specificity intensifies gratitude

WHIMSICAL

Embrace your holiness.

Harmony Day (AUS)

WHAT DO I WANT
THE MOST?

SOUL PROMPT ... I am

SCHEDULE ... reframe "obligations" into "choices"

:

:

:

:

:

:

:

:

:

:

:

:

:

:

3 THINGS ... that are moving your life forward

TO-DO ... prioritize pleasure

STOP DOING ... work for Love

WANT TO CHANGE ... the solution will come

GRATITUDE ... note WHY you're grateful

If you tone it down, life can't hear you.

PROLIFIC

MY CORE DESIRED FEELINGS

WHAT I WILL DO TO FEEL
THE WAY I WANT TO FEEL

SOUL PROMPT ... I will be

SCHEDULE ... does it light you up?

3 THINGS ... that are doable today

TO-DO ... less striving, more living

STOP DOING ... don't take any crap

WANT TO CHANGE ... clarity is power

GRATITUDE ... puts everything into perspective

LIGHTNESS

You're going to get off course. That's part of the journey. Just come back to it.

MY CORE DESIRED FEELINGS

W H
T H

SOUL PROMPT ... today, my heart feels

SCHEDULE ... respect yourself

:

:

:

:

:

:

:

:

:

:

:

:

:

:

3 THINGS ... that matter most

TO-DO ... the WHOLE point is to feel good

STOP DOING ... does it feel light or heavy?

WANT TO CHANGE ... why should it be different?

GRATITUDE ... challenges are teachers

Choosing the "easy way" is smart, efficient and a fantastic form of self-compassion.

INNOVATION

MY CORE DESIRED FEELINGS

WHAT I WILL DO TO FEEL
THE WAY I WANT TO FEEL

SOUL PROMPT ... I don't want to

SCHEDULE ... joy expands time

3 THINGS... because focus creates momentum

:
:
:
:

TO-DO ... it's your life. YOUR life. Your LIFE.

:
:
:
:
:

STOP DOING ... freedom is your birthright

:
:
:

WANT TO CHANGE ... naming it is liberating

GRATITUDE ... expands your consciousness

INTEGRITY

Take less shit. Way less.

WHAT
THE

TO-DO ... make choices that liberate you   **TO-DO** ... your desires are sacred

REFLECT ... enthusiasm saves lives   **ENVISION** ... I'm devoted to

Identify with light.

KICK-ASS

WHAT I WILL DO TO FEEL
THE WAY I WANT TO FEEL

SOUL PROMPT ... I will

SCHEDULE ... simplicity is freedom

:
:
:
:
:
:
:
:
:
:
:
:
:
:

3 THINGS ... get this done and the rest is a bonus

TO-DO ... keep your soul on the agenda

STOP DOING ... *No* makes way for *Yes*

WANT TO CHANGE ... claim it. Tame it.

GRATITUDE ... specificity intensifies gratitude

OPEN-HEARTED

Clarity creates simplicity.

WHAT
THE

SOUL PROMPT ... I'm reaching for

SCHEDULE ... reframe "obligations" into "choices"

:
:
:
:
:
:
:
:
:
:
:
:
:
:

3 THINGS ... that are moving your life forward

TO-DO ... prioritize pleasure

STOP DOING ... work for Love

WANT TO CHANGE ... the solution will come

GRATITUDE ... note WHY you're grateful

Make stuff that feels good to make.

ADVENTUROUS

MY CORE DESIRED FEELINGS

WHAT I WILL DO TO FEEL
THE WAY I WANT TO FEEL

SOUL PROMPT ... I'm overflowing with

SCHEDULE ... does it light you up?

3 THINGS ... that are doable today

TO-DO ... less striving, more living

STOP DOING ... don't take any crap

WANT TO CHANGE ... clarity is power

GRATITUDE ... puts everything into perspective

LIFE-GIVING

Take radical responsibility.

MY CORE DESIRED FEELINGS

WHAT
THE

SOUL PROMPT ... today, my heart feels

SCHEDULE ... respect yourself

·
·
·
·
·
·
·
·
·
·
·
·
·

3 THINGS ... that matter most

TO-DO ... the WHOLE point is to feel good

STOP DOING ... does it feel light or heavy?

WANT TO CHANGE ... why should it be different?

GRATITUDE ... challenges are teachers

Consider the source.

BOUNTIFUL

MY CORE DESIRED FEELINGS

WHAT I WILL DO TO FEEL
THE WAY I WANT TO FEEL

SOUL PROMPT ... I embody

SCHEDULE ... joy expands time

- :
- :
- :
- :
- :
- :
- :
- :
- :
- :
- :
- :
- :
- :

3 THINGS ... because focus creates momentum

TO-DO ... it's your life. YOUR life. Your LIFE.

STOP DOING ... freedom is your birthright

WANT TO CHANGE ... naming it is liberating

GRATITUDE ... expands your consciousness

REPLENISHED

Synchronicity is the universe saying, YES!

IDEAS. DESIRES. WISDOM. ... your heart is genius

Consider it done.

COLOURFUL

APRIL
2017

bliss

blissful

cheerful

delight

delightful

ebullient

ecstasy

ecstatic

elation

euphoria

euphoric

joy

joyful

joyous

jubilant

lightheartedness

rapture

rapturous

MONDAY	TUESDAY	WEDNESDAY
WEEK 13		
3	4	5
WEEK 14		
Passover begins (evening) 10	O Full Moon 11	12
WEEK 15		
17	**Passover ends (evening)** 18	Sun enters Taurus 19
WEEK 16		
24	**ANZAC Day (AUS)** 25	● New Moon 26
WEEK 17		

THURSDAY	FRIDAY	SATURDAY	SUNDAY
		1	2
National Tartan Day (CAN) 6	7	8	Mercury goes retrograde 9
13	**Good Friday** 14	15	**Easter Sunday** 16
20	21	**Earth Day** 22	23
27	28	29	30

APRIL

APRIL 2017 MONTHLY CHECK-IN

My Core Desired Feelings:

Feelings inform your wellness, your creations, your wisdom. Tune in to the predominant and new feelings that are running through you these days.

My major intentions & goals for the year:

Revisit your vision. When your core desired feelings lead the way, both your goals and how you go after them become more satisfying. How are your goals a reflection of how you most want to feel?

To generate my CDFs through my intentions & goals, I will:

What will it take to fulfill your vision for the year? Evaluate, affirm, or adjust your to-dos and intentions according to what you think will generate your core desired feelings along the way.

SACRED

IDEAS. DESIRES. WISDOM. ... leave room for magic & meandering

NATURAL

SATURDAY April 1 | 2017

SUNDAY April 2 | 2017

WHAT I WILL DO TO FEEL
THE WAY I WANT TO FEEL

TO-DO ... make choices that liberate you

TO-DO ... your desires are sacred

REFLECT ... rest

ENVISION ... don't hold back

ORGASMIC

Desire leads to truth.

WHAT
THE

SOUL PROMPT ... where do you hide?

SCHEDULE ... simplicity is freedom

:

:

:

:

:

:

:

:

:

:

:

:

:

:

3 THINGS ... get this done and the rest is a bonus

TO-DO ... keep your soul on the agenda

STOP DOING ... *No makes way for Yes*

WANT TO CHANGE ... claim it. Tame it.

GRATITUDE ... specificity intensifies gratitude

Giving is the antidote to emptiness.

OVERJOYED

MY CORE DESIRED FEELINGS

WHAT I WILL DO TO FEEL
THE WAY I WANT TO FEEL

SOUL PROMPT ... I'm on fire to

SCHEDULE ... reframe "obligations" into "choices"

: ....
: ....
: ....
: ....
: ....
: ....
: ....
: ....
: ....
: ....
: ....
: ....

3 THINGS ... that are moving your life forward

....
....
....

TO-DO ... prioritize pleasure

....
....
....
....
....
....

STOP DOING ... work for Love

WANT TO CHANGE ... the solution will come

GRATITUDE ... note WHY you're grateful

ALLURING

Are you expanding or contracting? (Note: expanding is often ideal.)

MY CORE DESIRED FEELINGS

WHAT
THE

SOUL PROMPT ... I am trying to impress

SCHEDULE ... does it light you up?

- :
- :
- :
- :
- :
- :
- :
- :
- :
- :
- :
- :
- :
- :

3 THINGS ... that are doable today

TO-DO ... less striving, more living

STOP DOING ... don't take any crap

WANT TO CHANGE ... clarity is power

GRATITUDE ... puts everything into perspective

Your scars are someone else's sign of hope.

LION-HEARTED

MY CORE DESIRED FEELINGS

WHAT I WILL DO TO FEEL
THE WAY I WANT TO FEEL

SOUL PROMPT ... today, my heart feels

SCHEDULE ... respect yourself

:
:
:
:
:
:
:
:
:
:
:
:
:

3 THINGS ... that matter most

TO-DO ... the WHOLE point is to feel good

STOP DOING ... does it feel light or heavy?

WANT TO CHANGE ... why should it be different?

GRATITUDE ... challenges are teachers

BOUNDLESS

Have the courage to enjoy it.

SOUL PROMPT ... what's different about me is that

SCHEDULE ... joy expands time

:

:

:

:

:

:

:

:

:

:

:

:

:

:

3 THINGS ... because focus creates momentum

TO-DO ... it's your life. YOUR life. Your LIFE.

STOP DOING ... freedom is your birthright

WANT TO CHANGE ... naming it is liberating

GRATITUDE ... expands your consciousness

Be the exception.

SEEN

WHAT I WILL DO TO FEEL
THE WAY I WANT TO FEEL

TO-DO ... make choices that liberate you

TO-DO ... your desires are sacred

REFLECT ... this week I learned

ENVISION ... what do you *really* want to happen?

INCOMPARABLE

Ponder the beauty of possibility.

MONDAY April 10 | 2017

Passover begins (evening)

WHAT
THE WAY

SOUL PROMPT ... what would going wild look like for you?

SCHEDULE ... simplicity is freedom

:

:

:

:

:

:

:

:

:

:

:

:

:

:

3 THINGS ... get this done and the rest is a bonus

TO-DO ... keep your soul on the agenda

STOP DOING ... *No makes way for Yes*

WANT TO CHANGE ... claim it. Tame it.

GRATITUDE ... specificity intensifies gratitude

Spill blessings every every everywhere.

LOYAL

MY CORE DESIRED FEELINGS

WHAT I WILL DO TO FEEL
THE WAY I WANT TO FEEL

SOUL PROMPT ... I stand for

SCHEDULE ... reframe "obligations" into "choices"

:
:
:
:
:
:
:
:
:
:
:
:
:
:

3 THINGS ... that are moving your life forward

TO-DO ... prioritize pleasure

STOP DOING ... work for Love

WANT TO CHANGE ... the solution will come

GRATITUDE ... note WHY you're grateful

MYSTICAL

Don't force yourself to be interested. It could cost you years.

WHAT WILL BE
THE CHANGE

SOUL PROMPT ... what do you do even though you don't want to?

SCHEDULE ... does it light you up?

:

:

:

:

:

:

:

:

:

:

:

:

:

3 THINGS ... that are doable today

TO-DO ... less striving, more living

STOP DOING ... don't take any crap

WANT TO CHANGE ... clarity is power

GRATITUDE ... puts everything into perspective

It's not about ascending – it's about centring.

IMMERSED

MY CORE DESIRED FEELINGS

WHAT I WILL DO TO FEEL
THE WAY I WANT TO FEEL

SOUL PROMPT ... today, my heart feels

SCHEDULE ... respect yourself

3 THINGS ... that matter most

TO-DO ... the WHOLE point is to feel good

STOP DOING ... does it feel light or heavy?

WANT TO CHANGE ... why should it be different?

GRATITUDE ... challenges are teachers

PROFOUND

Procrastination can be a form of intuition.

Good Friday

WHAT I LOVE ABOUT
THE WEEKEND

SOUL PROMPT ... I value

SCHEDULE ... joy expands time

:
:
:
:
:
:
:
:
:
:
:
:
:
:

3 THINGS ... because focus creates momentum

TO-DO ... it's your life. YOUR life. Your LIFE.

STOP DOING ... freedom is your birthright

WANT TO CHANGE ... naming it is liberating

GRATITUDE ... expands your consciousness

your heart is genius

COMFORTABLE

SATURDAY April 15 | 2017

SUNDAY April 16 | 2017
Easter Sunday

WHAT I WILL DO TO FEEL
THE WAY I WANT TO FEEL

TO-DO ... make choices that liberate you

TO-DO ... your desires are sacred

REFLECT ... what's true for you?

ENVISION ... let it be easy

VISIBLE

Your freedom is an urgent matter.

MY CORE DESIRED FEELINGS

SOUL PROMPT ... three things that bring me alive

SCHEDULE ... simplicity is freedom

:

:

:

:

:

:

:

:

:

:

:

:

:

:

WANT TO CHANGE ... claim it. Tame it.

3 THINGS ... get this done and the rest is a bonus

TO-DO ... keep your soul on the agenda

STOP DOING ... *No makes way for Yes*

GRATITUDE ... specificity intensifies gratitude

Put down your shield and stand in the rain of blessings.

BRIGHT FAITH

Passover ends (evening)

WHAT I WILL DO TO FEEL
THE WAY I WANT TO FEEL

SOUL PROMPT ... when I'm feeling strong, I

SCHEDULE ... reframe "obligations" into "choices"

- :
- :
- :
- :
- :
- :
- :
- :
- :
- :
- :
- :
- :
- :

3 THINGS ... that are moving your life forward

TO-DO ... prioritize pleasure

STOP DOING ... work for Love

WANT TO CHANGE ... the solution will come

GRATITUDE ... note WHY you're grateful

TUNED IN

What would your life be like if you only did what was easy?

MY CORE DESIRED FEELINGS

WHAT WILL DOI FEEL
THE WASH OF TOTALLY?

SOUL PROMPT ... the best advice you have ever been given

SCHEDULE ... does it light you up?

:
:
:
:
:
:
:
:
:
:
:
:
:
:

3 THINGS ... that are doable today

TO-DO ... less striving, more living

STOP DOING ... don't take any crap

WANT TO CHANGE ... clarity is power

GRATITUDE ... puts everything into perspective

The journey to sovereignty is usually pretty messy.

IN FLOW

MY CORE DESIRED FEELINGS

WHAT I WILL DO TO FEEL
THE WAY I WANT TO FEEL

SOUL PROMPT ... today, my heart feels

SCHEDULE ... respect yourself

- :
- :
- :
- :
- :
- :
- :
- :
- :
- :
- :
- :
- :
- :

3 THINGS ... that matter most

TO-DO ... the WHOLE point is to feel good

STOP DOING ... does it feel light or heavy?

WANT TO CHANGE ... why should it be different?

GRATITUDE ... challenges are teachers

RENEWED

It just takes one.

WHAT
THE

SOUL PROMPT ... I would describe my leadership style as

SCHEDULE ... joy expands time

3 THINGS ... because focus creates momentum

:

:

:

:

TO-DO ... it's your life. YOUR life. Your LIFE.

:

:

:

:

:

:

STOP DOING ... freedom is your birthright

:

:

:

:

WANT TO CHANGE ... naming it is liberating

GRATITUDE ... expands your consciousness

Long for another way.

PLEASURE

WHAT I WILL DO TO FEEL
THE WAY I WANT TO FEEL

TO-DO ... make choices that liberate you

TO-DO ... your desires are sacred

REFLECT ... speak up

ENVISION ... your soul is rooting for you

INFINITE

Why would you want to delay gratification?

WHAT WOULD IT BE LIKE
THE WAY TOGETHER FREE

SOUL PROMPT ... I'm against

SCHEDULE ... simplicity is freedom

- :
- :
- :
- :
- :
- :
- :
- :
- :
- :
- :
- :
- :
- :

3 THINGS ... get this done and the rest is a bonus

TO-DO ... keep your soul on the agenda

STOP DOING ... *No makes way for Yes*

WANT TO CHANGE ... claim it. Tame it.

GRATITUDE ... specificity intensifies gratitude

Ecstasy is your birthright.

TRIUMPHANT

TUESDAY April 25 | 2017

ANZAC Day (AUS)

MY CORE DESIRED FEELINGS

WHAT I WILL DO TO FEEL
THE WAY I WANT TO FEEL

SOUL PROMPT ... my joy comes from

SCHEDULE ... reframe "obligations" into "choices"

3 THINGS ... that are moving your life forward

TO-DO ... prioritize pleasure

STOP DOING ... work for Love

WANT TO CHANGE ... the solution will come

GRATITUDE ... note WHY you're grateful

INVIGORATED

Be someone's Yes.

MY CORE DESIRED FEELINGS

WH
THE

SOUL PROMPT ... when in doubt, I

SCHEDULE ... does it light you up?

⋮

⋮

⋮

⋮

⋮

⋮

⋮

⋮

⋮

⋮

⋮

⋮

⋮

⋮

3 THINGS ... that are doable today

TO-DO ... less striving, more living

STOP DOING ... don't take any crap

WANT TO CHANGE ... clarity is power

GRATITUDE ... puts everything into perspective

The deeper your self love, the greater your protection.

IRREPRESSIBLE

MY CORE DESIRED FEELINGS

WHAT I WILL DO TO FEEL
THE WAY I WANT TO FEEL

SOUL PROMPT ... today, my heart feels

SCHEDULE ... respect yourself

:
:
:
:
:
:
:
:
:
:
:
:
:
:

3 THINGS ... that matter most

TO-DO ... the WHOLE point is to feel good

STOP DOING ... does it feel light or heavy?

WANT TO CHANGE ... why should it be different?

GRATITUDE ... challenges are teachers

PRESENCE

If you don't feel it, don't fake it.

SOUL PROMPT ... I feel vulnerable when

SCHEDULE ... joy expands time

:
:
:
:
:
:
:
:
:
:
:
:
:
:

3 THINGS ... because focus creates momentum

TO-DO ... it's your life. YOUR life. Your LIFE.

STOP DOING ... freedom is your birthright

WANT TO CHANGE ... naming it is liberating

GRATITUDE ... expands your consciousness

Focus on the energy of the solution.

DEEPLY CONNECTED

WHAT I WILL DO TO FEEL
THE WAY I WANT TO FEEL

TO-DO ... make choices that liberate you

TO-DO ... your desires are sacred

REFLECT ... enthusiasm saves lives

ENVISION ... I'm devoted to

EXPRESSIVE

Loving yourself may mean that you appear to be unloving to others at times.

Talk about how you feel.

CLARITY

MAY
2017

cherishing

divine feminine

elegance

elegant

feminine

femininity

gentle

goddess

nurtured

nurturing

open

open-hearted

receiving

receptive

vibrant

MAY

MONDAY	TUESDAY	WEDNESDAY
May Day/Beltane 1	2	Mercury turns direct 3
WEEK 18		
8	9	○ Full Moon 10
WEEK 19		
15	16	17
WEEK 20		
Victoria Day (CAN) 22	23	24
WEEK 21		
Memorial Day (US) 29	30	31
WEEK 22		

THURSDAY	FRIDAY	SATURDAY	SUNDAY
4	**Cinco de Mayo** 5	6	7
11	12	13	**Mother's Day** 14
18	19	Sun enters Gemini 20	21
● New Moon 25	26	**Ramadan begins** 27	28

MAY

MAY 2017 MONTHLY CHECK-IN

My Core Desired Feelings:

Feelings inform your wellness, your creations, your wisdom. Tune in to the predominant and new feelings that are running through you these days.

My major intentions & goals for the year:

Revisit your vision. When your core desired feelings lead the way, both your goals and how you go after them become more satisfying. How are your goals a reflection of how you most want to feel?

To generate my CDFs through my intentions & goals, I will:

What will it take to fulfill your vision for the year? Evaluate, affirm, or adjust your to-dos and intentions according to what you think will generate your core desired feelings along the way.

FLOWING

IDEAS. DESIRES. WISDOM. ... feel free

SIMPLICITY

MONDAY May 1 | 2017
May Day/Beltane

MY CORE DESIRED FEELINGS

WHAT I WILL DO TO FEEL
THE WAY I WANT TO FEEL

SOUL PROMPT ... I need to have a good cry about

SCHEDULE ... simplicity is freedom

:
:
:
:
:
:
:
:
:
:
:
:
:
:

3 THINGS ... get this done and the rest is a bonus

TO-DO ... keep your soul on the agenda

STOP DOING ... *No* makes way for *Yes*

WANT TO CHANGE ... claim it. Tame it.

GRATITUDE ... specificity intensifies gratitude

SYNCHRONOUS

Let your heart break open.

SOUL PROMPT ... it hurts but I'm gonna

SCHEDULE ... reframe "obligations" into "choices"

3 THINGS ... that are moving your life forward

   :

   :

   :

   :

TO-DO ... prioritize pleasure

   :

   :

   :

   :

   :

   :

   :

STOP DOING ... work for Love

   :

   :

   :

WANT TO CHANGE ... the solution will come

GRATITUDE ... note WHY you're grateful

Focus. It hurts so good.

SOUL

MY CORE DESIRED FEELINGS

WHAT I WILL DO TO FEEL
THE WAY I WANT TO FEEL

SOUL PROMPT ... my most regular waking thought is

SCHEDULE ... does it light you up?

3 THINGS ... that are doable today

TO-DO ... less striving, more living

STOP DOING ... don't take any crap

WANT TO CHANGE ... clarity is power

GRATITUDE ... puts everything into perspective

CHILDLIKE

Work works better if you enjoy it.

WHAT
THE

SOUL PROMPT ... today, my heart feels

SCHEDULE ... respect yourself   **3 THINGS** ... that matter most

:

:

:

:   **TO-DO** ... the WHOLE point is to feel good

:

:

:

:

:

:

:   **STOP DOING** ... does it feel light or heavy?

:

:

:

WANT TO CHANGE ... why should it be different?   **GRATITUDE** ... challenges are teachers

You've got to say a lot of noes so you can say the most important Yeses.

FIERCE LOVE

MY CORE DESIRED FEELINGS

WHAT I WILL DO TO FEEL
THE WAY I WANT TO FEEL

SOUL PROMPT ... I'm greedy with

SCHEDULE ... joy expands time

:
:
:
:
:
:
:
:
:
:
:
:
:
:

3 THINGS ... because focus creates momentum

TO-DO ... it's your life. YOUR life. Your LIFE.

STOP DOING ... freedom is your birthright

WANT TO CHANGE ... naming it is liberating

GRATITUDE ... expands your consciousness

FULLY EXPRESSED

To innovate, you need to lighten your load. Constantly.

SATURDAY May 6 | 2017   SUNDAY May 7 | 2017

TO-DO ... make choices that liberate you   **TO-DO** ... your desires are sacred

REFLECT ... rest   **ENVISION** ... don't hold back

Bliss isn't something you work for. It's something you follow.

EFFORTLESS

MY CORE DESIRED FEELINGS

WHAT I WILL DO TO FEEL
THE WAY I WANT TO FEEL

SOUL PROMPT ... I've forgotten how

SCHEDULE ... simplicity is freedom

:
:
:
:
:
:
:
:
:
:
:
:
:
:

3 THINGS ... get this done and the rest is a bonus

TO-DO ... keep your soul on the agenda

STOP DOING ... *No* makes way for *Yes*

WANT TO CHANGE ... claim it. Tame it.

GRATITUDE ... specificity intensifies gratitude

COSMIC

Art involves risk.

WHAT I LOVE ABOUT
THE WAY I LIVE

SOUL PROMPT ... I want more more more

SCHEDULE ... reframe "obligations" into "choices"

:

:

:

:

:

:

:

:

:

:

:

:

:

:

3 THINGS ... that are moving your life forward

TO-DO ... prioritize pleasure

STOP DOING ... work for Love

WANT TO CHANGE ... the solution will come

GRATITUDE ... note WHY you're grateful

Ideas, action, creation, prosperity.

BALANCED

MY CORE DESIRED FEELINGS

WHAT I WILL DO TO FEEL
THE WAY I WANT TO FEEL

SOUL PROMPT ... five words about money

SCHEDULE ... does it light you up?

3 THINGS ... that are doable today

TO-DO ... less striving, more living

STOP DOING ... don't take any crap

WANT TO CHANGE ... clarity is power

GRATITUDE ... puts everything into perspective

TRANQUIL

Wide open space = deeper creativity.

MY CORE DESIRED FEELINGS

SOUL PROMPT ... today, my heart feels

SCHEDULE ... respect yourself

:
:
:
:
:
:
:
:
:
:
:
:
:

3 THINGS ... that matter most

TO-DO ... the WHOLE point is to feel good

STOP DOING ... does it feel light or heavy?

WANT TO CHANGE ... why should it be different?

GRATITUDE ... challenges are teachers

Boundaries get tested. Expect it. That's why they're "boundaries" and not open doors.

NURTURED

MY CORE DESIRED FEELINGS

WHAT I WILL DO TO FEEL
THE WAY I WANT TO FEEL

SOUL PROMPT ... I feel confident when

SCHEDULE ... joy expands time

:
:
:
:
:
:
:
:
:
:
:
:
:
:

3 THINGS ... because focus creates momentum

TO-DO ... it's your life. YOUR life. Your LIFE.

STOP DOING ... freedom is your birthright

WANT TO CHANGE ... naming it is liberating

GRATITUDE ... expands your consciousness

ENDLESS

You are so capable of frequent bliss.

Mother's Day

WHAT IF I LED FROM
THE WAY I FEEL?

TO-DO ... make choices that liberate you

....

....

....

....

....

REFLECT ... this week I learned

TO-DO ... your desires are sacred

ENVISION ... what do you really want to happen?

Let there be space between you and your wish so fulfillment can pour in.

POETIC

MY CORE DESIRED FEELINGS

WILL DO TO FEEL
AS I WANT TO FEEL

SOUL PROMPT . . . . calms me.

SCHEDULE ... simplicity is freedom

- :
- :
- :
- :
- :
- :
- :
- :
- :
- :
- :
- :
- :

3 THINGS ... get this done and the rest is a bonus

TO-DO ... keep your soul on the agenda

STOP DOING ... *No* makes way for *Yes*

WANT TO CHANGE ... claim it. Tame it.

GRATITUDE ... specificity intensifies gratitude

IMAGINATIVE

Miracles happen – all the time.

MY CORE DESIRED FEELINGS

SOUL PROMPT ... I see

SCHEDULE ... reframe "obligations" into "choices"

:

:

:

:

:

:

:

:

:

:

:

:

:

:

WANT TO CHANGE ... the solution will come

3 THINGS ... that are moving your life forward

TO-DO ... prioritize pleasure

STOP DOING ... work for Love

GRATITUDE ... note WHY you're grateful

Honour your body and it will help you be even more creative.

KARMIC

MY CORE DESIRED FEELINGS

WHAT I WILL DO TO FEEL
THE WAY I WANT TO FEEL

SOUL PROMPT ... I feel anxious when

SCHEDULE ... does it light you up?

- :
- :
- :
- :
- :
- :
- :
- :
- :
- :
- :
- :
- :
- :

3 THINGS ... that are doable today

TO-DO ... less striving, more living

STOP DOING ... don't take any crap

WANT TO CHANGE ... clarity is power

GRATITUDE ... puts everything into perspective

RESPECTED

When you trust that your pain is/was real, you'll trust your joy more.

MY CORE DESIRED FEELINGS

WHAT
THE

SOUL PROMPT ... today, my heart feels

SCHEDULE ... respect yourself

:

:

:

:

:

:

:

:

:

:

:

:

:

:

3 THINGS ... that matter most

TO-DO ... the WHOLE point is to feel good

STOP DOING ... does it feel light or heavy?

WANT TO CHANGE ... why should it be different?

GRATITUDE ... challenges are teachers

Grant yourself permission.

HEALED

MY CORE DESIRED FEELINGS

THIS I WILL DO TO FEEL
THE WAY I WANT TO FEEL

SOUL PROMPT ... I'm so disappointed with

SCHEDULE ... joy expands time

- :
- :
- :
- :
- :
- :
- :
- :
- :
- :
- :
- :
- :
- :

3 THINGS ... because focus creates momentum

TO-DO ... it's your life. YOUR life. Your LIFE.

STOP DOING ... freedom is your birthright

WANT TO CHANGE ... naming it is liberating

GRATITUDE ... expands your consciousness

SOUL-CENTRED

Disappointments can be openings.

TO-DO ... make choices that liberate you

TO-DO ... your desires are sacred

REFLECT ... what's true for you?

ENVISION ... let it be easy

Tell people how you feel.

AWAKENED

WHAT I WILL DO TO FEEL
THE WAY I WANT TO FEEL

SOUL PROMPT ... I cherish

SCHEDULE ... simplicity is freedom

:
:
:
:
:
:
:
:
:
:
:
:
:
:

3 THINGS ... get this done and the rest is a bonus

TO-DO ... keep your soul on the agenda

STOP DOING ... *No* makes way for *Yes*

WANT TO CHANGE ... claim it. Tame it.

GRATITUDE ... specificity intensifies gratitude

SOFTNESS

Feel into your future.

TUESDAY May 23 | 2017

WHAT IS BLOOMING
THE WAY

SOUL PROMPT ... I connect with

SCHEDULE ... reframe "obligations" into "choices"

:
:
:
:
:
:
:
:
:
:
:
:
:
:

3 THINGS ... that are moving your life forward

TO-DO ... prioritize pleasure

STOP DOING ... work for Love

WANT TO CHANGE ... the solution will come

GRATITUDE ... note WHY you're grateful

Stand your ground, it's sacred.

CHEERFUL

MY CORE DESIRED FEELINGS

WHAT I WILL DO TO FEEL THE WAY I WANT TO FEEL

SOUL PROMPT ... three words to describe your anger

SCHEDULE ... does it light you up?

- :
- :
- :
- :
- :
- :
- :
- :
- :
- :
- :
- :
- :
- :

3 THINGS ... that are doable today

TO-DO ... less striving, more living

STOP DOING ... don't take any crap

WANT TO CHANGE ... clarity is power

GRATITUDE ... puts everything into perspective

VITAL

You've got a new story to write. And it looks nothing like your past.

MY CORE DESIRED FEELINGS

SOUL PROMPT ... today, my heart feels

SCHEDULE ... respect yourself

:

:

:

:

:

:

:

:

:

:

:

:

:

3 THINGS ... that matter most

TO-DO ... the WHOLE point is to feel good

STOP DOING ... does it feel light or heavy?

WANT TO CHANGE ... why should it be different?

GRATITUDE ... challenges are teachers

Pleasure is Power

AT HOME

MY CORE DESIRED FEELINGS

WHAT I WILL DO TO FEEL
THE WAY I WANT TO FEEL

SOUL PROMPT ... three things that weigh you down

SCHEDULE ... joy expands time

:
:
:
:
:
:
:
:
:
:
:
:
:

WANT TO CHANGE ... naming it is liberating

3 THINGS ... because focus creates momentum

TO-DO ... it's your life. YOUR life. Your LIFE.

STOP DOING ... freedom is your birthright

GRATITUDE ... expands your consciousness

SPARK

When faced with a choice between a deadline and a friend, almost always choose the friend.

Ramadan begins

WHAT IF WE WERE
THE WATER THIS

TO-DO ... make choices that liberate you

TO-DO ... your desires are sacred

REFLECT ... speak up

ENVISION ... your soul is rooting for you

You are free to choose.

FERVENT

MONDAY May 29 | 2017
Memorial Day (US)

MY CORE DESIRED FEELINGS

WHAT I WILL DO TO FEEL
THE WAY I WANT TO FEEL

SOUL PROMPT ... at the centre of my life

SCHEDULE ... simplicity is freedom

:
:
:
:
:
:
:
:
:
:
:
:
:
:

3 THINGS ... get this done and the rest is a bonus

TO-DO ... keep your soul on the agenda

STOP DOING ... *No* makes way for *Yes*

WANT TO CHANGE ... claim it. Tame it.

GRATITUDE ... specificity intensifies gratitude

DIVINE GRACE

Believe what you want – because what you believe will influence your future.

SOUL PROMPT ... I aim to

SCHEDULE ... reframe "obligations" into "choices"

:

:

:

:

:

:

:

:

:

:

:

:

:

:

3 THINGS ... that are moving your life forward

TO-DO ... prioritize pleasure

STOP DOING ... work for Love

WANT TO CHANGE ... the solution will come

GRATITUDE ... note WHY you're grateful

Protect your heart so you can keep it wide open.

SURE

WHAT I WILL DO TO FEEL
THE WAY I WANT TO FEEL

SOUL PROMPT ... I'm giving

SCHEDULE ... does it light you up?

:
:
:
:
:
:
:
:
:
:
:
:
:
:

3 THINGS ... that are doable today

TO-DO ... less striving, more living

STOP DOING ... don't take any crap

WANT TO CHANGE ... clarity is power

GRATITUDE ... puts everything into perspective

ELECTRIC

You are worthy of your desires.

IDEAS. DESIRES. WISDOM. ... take up space

Be proud of what you Love.

RELAXED

JUNE
2017

artful

artistic

creating

creative

genius

gifted

innovative

inspirational

inspired

inspiring

inventive

magic

magical

original

play

playful

seeing

seen

visionary

MONDAY	TUESDAY	WEDNESDAY
WEEK 22		
5	**D-Day** 6	7
WEEK 23		
Queen's Birthday (AUS) 12	13	14
WEEK 24		
19	20	**Summer Solstice/ Litha National Aboriginal Day (CAN)** 21 Sun enters Cancer
WEEK 25		
26	27	28
WEEK 26		

THURSDAY	FRIDAY	SATURDAY	SUNDAY
1	2	3	4
8	○ Full Moon 9	10	11
15	16	17	Father's Day 18
22	● New Moon 23	24	Ramadan ends 25
29	30		

JUNE 2017 MONTHLY CHECK-IN

My Core Desired Feelings:

Feelings inform your wellness, your creations, your wisdom. Tune in to the predominant and new feelings that are running through you these days.

My major intentions & goals for the year:

Revisit your vision. When your core desired feelings lead the way, both your goals and how you go after them become more satisfying. How are your goals a reflection of how you most want to feel?

To generate my CDFs through my intentions & goals, I will:

What will it take to fulfill your vision for the year? Evaluate, affirm, or adjust your to-dos and intentions according to what you think will generate your core desired feelings along the way.

ENTHRALLED

IDEAS. DESIRES. WISDOM. ... your heart is genius

IRRESISTABLE

WHAT I WILL DO TO FEEL
THE WAY I WANT TO FEEL

SOUL PROMPT ... for the sake of my sanity, I am going to let this slip

SCHEDULE ... respect yourself

3 THINGS ... that matter most

TO-DO ... the WHOLE point is to feel good

STOP DOING ... does it feel light or heavy?

WANT TO CHANGE ... why should it be different?

GRATITUDE ... challenges are teachers

ANCHORED

If you want to do great things, striving for "balance" is a losing game.

WHAT
THE

SOUL PROMPT ... today, my heart feels

SCHEDULE ... joy expands time   **3 THINGS** ... because focus creates momentum

:

:

:

:   **TO-DO** ... it's your life. YOUR life. Your LIFE.

:

:

:

:

:

:

:   **STOP DOING** ... freedom is your birthright

:

:

:

WANT TO CHANGE ... naming it is liberating   **GRATITUDE** ... expands your consciousness

MIGHTY

Bring it up.

WHAT I WILL DO TO FEEL
THE WAY I WANT TO FEEL

TO-DO ... make choices that liberate you

TO-DO ... your desires are sacred

REFLECT ... enthusiasm saves lives

ENVISION ... I'm devoted to

BRIMMING

Let your voice ride on your breath.

WH ... ...
THE ...

SOUL PROMPT ... I feel the most free when

SCHEDULE ... simplicity is freedom

:

:

:

:

:

:

:

:

:

:

:

:

:

:

3 THINGS ... get this done and the rest is a bonus

TO-DO ... keep your soul on the agenda

STOP DOING ... *No makes way for Yes*

WANT TO CHANGE ... claim it. Tame it.

GRATITUDE ... specificity intensifies gratitude

The light never lies.

LIMITLESS

MY CORE DESIRED FEELINGS

WHAT I WILL DO TO FEEL
THE WAY I WANT TO FEEL

SOUL PROMPT ... I think my greatest talent is

SCHEDULE ... reframe "obligations" into "choices"

- :
- :
- :
- :
- :
- :
- :
- :
- :
- :
- :
- :
- :
- :

3 THINGS ... that are moving your life forward

TO-DO ... prioritize pleasure

STOP DOING ... work for Love

WANT TO CHANGE ... the solution will come

GRATITUDE ... note WHY you're grateful

BELOVED

Only seek to be more of yourself.

MY CORE DESIRED FEELINGS

SOUL PROMPT ... three reasons I am beautiful

SCHEDULE ... does it light you up?

:

:

:

:

:

:

:

:

:

:

:

:

:

:

3 THINGS ... that are doable today

TO-DO ... less striving, more living

STOP DOING ... don't take any crap

WANT TO CHANGE ... clarity is power

GRATITUDE ... puts everything into perspective

Joy is sexy.

OUTRAGEOUS

MY CORE DESIRED FEELINGS

WHAT I WILL DO TO FEEL
THE WAY I WANT TO FEEL

SOUL PROMPT ... today, my heart feels

SCHEDULE ... respect yourself

:
:
:
:
:
:
:
:
:
:
:
:
:

3 THINGS ... that matter most

TO-DO ... the WHOLE point is to feel good

STOP DOING ... does it feel light or heavy?

WANT TO CHANGE ... why should it be different?

GRATITUDE ... challenges are teachers

FREEDOM

if you declare that you'll figure it out, the possibilities are endless.

FRIDAY June 9 | 2017
○ Full Moon

MY CORE DESIRED FEELINGS

WHAT
THE

SOUL PROMPT ... I wish I were more

SCHEDULE ... joy expands time

:

:

:

:

:

:

:

:

:

:

:

:

:

:

3 THINGS ... because focus creates momentum

TO-DO ... it's your life. YOUR life. Your LIFE.

STOP DOING ... freedom is your birthright

WANT TO CHANGE ... naming it is liberating

GRATITUDE ... expands your consciousness

You're in charge of your own karma.

PRACTICAL

WHAT I WILL DO TO FEEL
THE WAY I WANT TO FEEL

TO-DO ... make choices that liberate you

TO-DO ... your desires are sacred

REFLECT ... rest

ENVISION ... don't hold back

MASTERFUL

Consider everything you've ever been thanked for.

MY CORE DESIRED FEELINGS

SOUL PROMPT ... I'm devoted to

SCHEDULE ... simplicity is freedom

:

:

:

:

:

:

:

:

:

:

:

:

:

:

3 THINGS ... get this done and the rest is a bonus

TO-DO ... keep your soul on the agenda

STOP DOING ... *No* makes way for *Yes*

WANT TO CHANGE ... claim it. Tame it.

GRATITUDE ... specificity intensifies gratitude

Create an ideal story of your future and tell it over and over again.

MAGNETIC

MY CORE DESIRED FEELINGS

WHAT I WILL DO TO FEEL
THE WAY I WANT TO FEEL

SOUL PROMPT ... I could be

SCHEDULE ... reframe "obligations" into "choices"

:
:
:
:
:
:
:
:
:
:
:
:
:
:

3 THINGS ... that are moving your life forward

TO-DO ... prioritize pleasure

STOP DOING ... work for Love

WANT TO CHANGE ... the solution will come

GRATITUDE ... note WHY you're grateful

ONENESS

Excuses repress clarity.

SOUL PROMPT ... the most encouraging thing someone could say to you right now would be

SCHEDULE ... does it light you up?

:

:

:

:

:

:

:

:

:

:

:

:

:

:

3 THINGS ... that are doable today

TO-DO ... less striving, more living

STOP DOING ... don't take any crap

WANT TO CHANGE ... clarity is power

GRATITUDE ... puts everything into perspective

Blessing. Curse. It's your call.

STRENGTH

WHAT I WILL DO TO FEEL
THE WAY I WANT TO FEEL

SOUL PROMPT ... today, my heart feels

SCHEDULE ... respect yourself

:
:
:
:
:
:
:
:
:
:
:
:
:
:

3 THINGS ... that matter most

TO-DO ... the WHOLE point is to feel good

STOP DOING ... does it feel light or heavy?

WANT TO CHANGE ... why should it be different?

GRATITUDE ... challenges are teachers

RESONANCE

Keep your heart open and the answer will show up.

SOUL PROMPT ... I feel loving when

SCHEDULE ... joy expands time

- :
- :
- :
- :
- :
- :
- :
- :
- :
- :
- :
- :
- :
- :

3 THINGS ... because focus creates momentum

TO-DO ... it's your life. YOUR life. Your LIFE.

STOP DOING ... freedom is your birthright

WANT TO CHANGE ... naming it is liberating

GRATITUDE ... expands your consciousness

If knowledge is power, then curiosity is the muscle.

ROMANCED

WHAT I WILL DO TO FEEL
THE WAY I WANT TO FEEL

TO-DO ... make choices that liberate you

TO-DO ... your desires are sacred

REFLECT ... this week I learned

ENVISION ... what do you *really* want to happen?

OTHERWORLDLY

dream of being amazed

MY CORE DESIRED FEELINGS

SOUL PROMPT ... I am burning

SCHEDULE ... simplicity is freedom

:
:
:
:
:
:
:
:
:
:
:
:
:
:

3 THINGS ... get this done and the rest is a bonus

TO-DO ... keep your soul on the agenda

STOP DOING ... *No makes way for Yes*

WANT TO CHANGE ... claim it. Tame it.

GRATITUDE ... specificity intensifies gratitude

Happiness is carbonated consciousness.

REMARKABLE

MY CORE DESIRED FEELINGS

WHAT I WILL DO TO FEEL
THE WAY I WANT TO FEEL

SOUL PROMPT ... I know I'm happy when

SCHEDULE ... reframe "obligations" into "choices"

- :
- :
- :
- :
- :
- :
- :
- :
- :
- :
- :
- :
- :

3 THINGS ... that are moving your life forward

TO-DO ... prioritize pleasure

STOP DOING ... work for Love

WANT TO CHANGE ... the solution will come

GRATITUDE ... note WHY you're grateful

VICTORIOUS

Focus on the infinite possibilities.

WEDNESDAY June 21 | 2017

Summer Solstice/Litha | National Aboriginal Day (CAN)
Sun enters Cancer

MY CORE DESIRED FEELINGS

SOUL PROMPT ... I'm comforted by

SCHEDULE ... does it light you up?

:

:

:

:

:

:

:

:

:

:

:

:

:

:

3 THINGS ... that are doable today

TO-DO ... less striving, more living

STOP DOING ... don't take any crap

WANT TO CHANGE ... clarity is power

GRATITUDE ... puts everything into perspective

Contrast is an excellent teacher.

EXHILARATED

MY CORE DESIRED FEELINGS

WHAT I WILL DO TO FEEL
THE WAY I WANT TO FEEL

SOUL PROMPT ... I'm a really good

SCHEDULE ... respect yourself

:
:
:
:
:
:
:
:
:
:
:
:
:

3 THINGS ... that matter most

TO-DO ... the WHOLE point is to feel good

STOP DOING ... does it feel light or heavy?

WANT TO CHANGE ... why should it be different?

GRATITUDE ... challenges are teachers

SENSUAL

A soft heart is stronger.

● New Moon

SOUL PROMPT ... I feel Loved when

SCHEDULE ... joy expands time

   :

   :

   :

   :

   :

   :

   :

   :

   :

   :

   :

   :

   :

   :

3 THINGS ... because focus creates momentum

TO-DO ... it's your life. YOUR life. Your LIFE.

STOP DOING ... freedom is your birthright

WANT TO CHANGE ... naming it is liberating

GRATITUDE ... expands your consciousness

Remember how fun it is to learn.

BLISS

WHAT I WILL DO TO FEEL
THE WAY I WANT TO FEEL

TO-DO ... make choices that liberate you

TO-DO ... your desires are sacred

REFLECT ... what's true for you?

ENVISION ... let it be easy

IN LOVE

Focus on your natural capacities.

MY CORE DESIRED FEELINGS

SOUL PROMPT ... my favourite way to express gratitude is

SCHEDULE ... simplicity is freedom

3 THINGS ... get this done and the rest is a bonus

:

:

:

:

TO-DO ... keep your soul on the agenda

:

:

:

:

:

:

:

STOP DOING ... *No* makes way for *Yes*

:

:

:

WANT TO CHANGE ... claim it. Tame it.

GRATITUDE ... specificity intensifies gratitude

Your heart...your heart...your heart is where it's at.

ALIVE

WHAT I WILL DO TO FEEL
THE WAY I WANT TO FEEL

SOUL PROMPT ... I am most looking forward to

SCHEDULE ... reframe "obligations" into "choices"

:
:
:
:
:
:
:
:
:
:
:
:
:
:

3 THINGS ... that are moving your life forward

TO-DO ... prioritize pleasure

STOP DOING ... work for Love

WANT TO CHANGE ... the solution will come

GRATITUDE ... note WHY you're grateful

JUBILANT

It's not a race.

WHAT
THE

SOUL PROMPT ... I need to shake up

SCHEDULE ... does it light you up?

:
:
:
:
:
:
:
:
:
:
:
:
:
:

3 THINGS ... that are doable today

TO-DO ... less striving, more living

STOP DOING ... don't take any crap

WANT TO CHANGE ... clarity is power

GRATITUDE ... puts everything into perspective

Aim to get better at what you're already great at. THAT's mastery.

CLEAN

WHAT I WILL DO TO FEEL
THE WAY I WANT TO FEEL

SOUL PROMPT ... today, my heart feels

SCHEDULE ... respect yourself

- :
- :
- :
- :
- :
- :
- :
- :
- :
- :
- :
- :
- :
- :

3 THINGS ... that matter most

TO-DO ... the WHOLE point is to feel good

STOP DOING ... does it feel light or heavy?

WANT TO CHANGE ... why should it be different?

GRATITUDE ... challenges are teachers

LIVELY

Obsession is essential to creativity.

WHAT
THE

SOUL PROMPT ... who is really inspiring you right now?

SCHEDULE ... joy expands time

:

:

:

:

:

:

:

:

:

:

:

:

:

:

3 THINGS ... because focus creates momentum

TO-DO ... it's your life. YOUR life. Your LIFE.

STOP DOING ... freedom is your birthright

WANT TO CHANGE ... naming it is liberating

GRATITUDE ... expands your consciousness

First thought, right answer.

JULY
2017

bountiful

flow

flowing

fluidity

free

freedom

liberation

liberty

natural

nature

power

powerful

sovereign

trust

trusting

MONDAY	TUESDAY	WEDNESDAY
WEEK 26		
3	**US Independence Day** 4	5
WEEK 27		
10	11	12
WEEK 28		
17	18	19
WEEK 29		
24	25	26
WEEK 30		
31		
WEEK 31		

THURSDAY	FRIDAY	SATURDAY	SUNDAY
		Canada Day 1	2
6	7	8 ○ Full Moon	9
13	**Bastille Day (FRA)** 14	15	16
20	21	Sun enters Leo 22	● New Moon 23
27	28	29	30

JULY 2017 MONTHLY CHECK-IN

My Core Desired Feelings:

Feelings inform your wellness, your creations, your wisdom. Tune in to the predominant and new feelings that are running through you these days.

My major intentions & goals for the year:

Revisit your vision. When your core desired feelings lead the way, both your goals and how you go after them become more satisfying. How are your goals a reflection of how you most want to feel?

To generate my CDFs through my intentions & goals, I will:

What will it take to fulfill your vision for the year? Evaluate, affirm, or adjust your to-dos and intentions according to what you think will generate your core desired feelings along the way.

NOBLE

IDEAS. DESIRES. WISDOM. ... leave room for magic & meandering

EVOLUTION

WHAT I WILL DO TO FEEL
THE WAY I WANT TO FEEL

TO-DO ... make choices that liberate you

TO-DO ... your desires are sacred

REFLECT ... speak up

ENVISION ... your soul is rooting for you

OVERFLOWING

We are all power brokers.

WHAT
THE WA

SOUL PROMPT ... I want to help

SCHEDULE ... simplicity is freedom

:
:
:
:
:
:
:
:
:
:
:
:
:
:

3 THINGS ... get this done and the rest is a bonus

TO-DO ... keep your soul on the agenda

STOP DOING ... *No makes way for Yes*

WANT TO CHANGE ... claim it. Tame it.

GRATITUDE ... specificity intensifies gratitude

Attend first to the divine and the work at hand becomes art.

INCANDESCENT

WHAT I WILL DO TO FEEL
THE WAY I WANT TO FEEL

SOUL PROMPT ... what are you creating?

SCHEDULE ... reframe "obligations" into "choices"

- :
- :
- :
- :
- :
- :
- :
- :
- :
- :
- :
- :
- :
- :

3 THINGS ... that are moving your life forward

TO-DO ... prioritize pleasure

STOP DOING ... work for Love

WANT TO CHANGE ... the solution will come

GRATITUDE ... note WHY you're grateful

SPIRIT

Desire drives deeds

WHAT
THE

SOUL PROMPT I really wish . . . . would call me.

SCHEDULE ... does it light you up?

:

:

:

:

:

:

:

:

:

:

:

:

:

:

3 THINGS ... that are doable today

TO-DO ... less striving, more living

STOP DOING ... don't take any crap

WANT TO CHANGE ... clarity is power

GRATITUDE ... puts everything into perspective

Your freedom is good for all of us.

FRESH

MY CORE DESIRED FEELINGS

WHAT I WILL DO TO FEEL
THE WAY I WANT TO FEEL

SOUL PROMPT ... today, my heart feels

SCHEDULE ... respect yourself

:
:
:
:
:
:
:
:
:
:
:
:
:

3 THINGS ... that matter most

TO-DO ... the WHOLE point is to feel good

STOP DOING ... does it feel light or heavy?

WANT TO CHANGE ... why should it be different?

GRATITUDE ... challenges are teachers

SEDUCTIVE

Dedicate your day to someone.

WHAT
THE WA

SOUL PROMPT ... my least favourite feeling

SCHEDULE ... joy expands time

:
:
:
:
:
:
:
:
:
:
:
:
:
:

3 THINGS ... because focus creates momentum

TO-DO ... it's your life. YOUR life. Your LIFE.

STOP DOING ... freedom is your birthright

WANT TO CHANGE ... naming it is liberating

GRATITUDE ... expands your consciousness

Generous people have more to give.

SATURDAY July 8 | 2017

SUNDAY July 9 | 2017
O Full Moon

WHAT I WILL DO TO FEEL
THE WAY I WANT TO FEEL

TO-DO ... make choices that liberate you

TO-DO ... your desires are sacred

REFLECT ... enthusiasm saves lives

ENVISION ... I'm devoted to

WHOLE

Know what you're afraid of.

WHAT
THE

SOUL PROMPT ... what I Love about being in Love

SCHEDULE ... simplicity is freedom

3 THINGS ... get this done and the rest is a bonus

:

:

:

:

TO-DO ... keep your soul on the agenda

:

:

:

:

:

:

STOP DOING ... *No* makes way for *Yes*

:

:

:

WANT TO CHANGE ... claim it. Tame it.

GRATITUDE ... specificity intensifies gratitude

You must have a relationship with death to live more fully.

UNLEASHED

MY CORE DESIRED FEELINGS

WHAT I WILL DO TO FEEL
THE WAY I WANT TO FEEL

SOUL PROMPT ... whose teaching has really influenced you?

SCHEDULE ... reframe "obligations" into "choices"

:
:
:
:
:
:
:
:
:
:
:
:
:

3 THINGS ... that are moving your life forward

TO-DO ... prioritize pleasure

STOP DOING ... work for Love

WANT TO CHANGE ... the solution will come

GRATITUDE ... note WHY you're grateful

SOFT

Keep statistics away from your dreams.

WHAT LIGHTS ME UP
THE WAY I WANT TO FEEL

SOUL PROMPT ... current favourite word

SCHEDULE ... does it light you up?

:
:
:
:
:
:
:
:
:
:
:
:
:
:

3 THINGS ... that are doable today

TO-DO ... less striving, more living

STOP DOING ... don't take any crap

WANT TO CHANGE ... clarity is power

GRATITUDE ... puts everything into perspective

Think of resentment as a mega-watt STOP sign. And stop.

WILDLY SENSUOUS

MY CORE DESIRED FEELINGS

WHAT I WILL DO TO FEEL
THE WAY I WANT TO FEEL

SOUL PROMPT ... today, my heart feels

SCHEDULE ... respect yourself

· :
· :
· :
· :
· :
· :
· :
· :
· :
· :
· :
· :
· :
· :

3 THINGS ... that matter most

TO-DO ... the WHOLE point is to feel good

STOP DOING ... does it feel light or heavy?

WANT TO CHANGE ... why should it be different?

GRATITUDE ... challenges are teachers

PERFECTION

Be kind. No matter what. (You can be kind and strong. You will need to be strong.)

MY CORE DESIRED FEELINGS

SOUL PROMPT ... what was your high point yesterday?

SCHEDULE ... joy expands time

:
:
:
:
:
:
:
:
:
:
:
:
:
:

3 THINGS ... because focus creates momentum

TO-DO ... it's your life. YOUR life. Your LIFE.

STOP DOING ... freedom is your birthright

WANT TO CHANGE ... naming it is liberating

GRATITUDE ... expands your consciousness

Focus on your superpowers.

SELFLESS

WHAT I WILL DO TO FEEL
THE WAY I WANT TO FEEL

TO-DO ... make choices that liberate you

TO-DO ... your desires are sacred

REFLECT ... rest

ENVISION ... don't hold back

MAGICAL

Move the way your soul likes to move.

MY CORE DESIRED FEELINGS

WHAT
THE

SOUL PROMPT ... I surrender to

SCHEDULE ... simplicity is freedom

3 THINGS ... get this done and the rest is a bonus

:

:

:

:

TO-DO ... keep your soul on the agenda

:

:

:

:

:

:

STOP DOING ... *No makes way for Yes*

:

:

:

WANT TO CHANGE ... claim it. Tame it.

GRATITUDE ... specificity intensifies gratitude

We create our lives through loving.

SOLID

MY CORE DESIRED FEELINGS

WILL DO TO FEEL
WANT TO FEEL

SOUL PROMPT ... I'm embracing

SCHEDULE ... reframe "obligations" into "choices"

:

:

:

:

:

:

:

:

:

:

:

:

:

3 THINGS ... that are moving your life forward

TO-DO ... prioritize pleasure

STOP DOING ... work for Love

WANT TO CHANGE ... the solution will come

GRATITUDE ... note WHY you're grateful

PRIMAL JOY

Strong preferences = deliberate creation.

SOUL PROMPT ... what relationship is really lighting you up right now

SCHEDULE ... does it light you up?

:

:

:

:

:

:

:

:

:

:

:

:

:

:

3 THINGS ... that are doable today

TO-DO ... less striving, more living

STOP DOING ... don't take any crap

WANT TO CHANGE ... clarity is power

GRATITUDE ... puts everything into perspective

Notice how you feel.

HOT

MY CORE DESIRED FEELINGS

WHAT I WILL DO TO FEEL
THE WAY I WANT TO FEEL

SOUL PROMPT ... today, my heart feels

SCHEDULE ... respect yourself

- :
- :
- :
- :
- :
- :
- :
- :
- :
- :
- :
- :
- :

3 THINGS ... that matter most

TO-DO ... the WHOLE point is to feel good

STOP DOING ... does it feel light or heavy?

WANT TO CHANGE ... why should it be different?

GRATITUDE ... challenges are teachers

REALIZED

Hang out with people you can easily adore, or at least respect.

WHAT
THE

SOUL PROMPT ... I know a lot about

SCHEDULE ... joy expands time

3 THINGS ... because focus creates momentum

:

:

:

:   **TO-DO** ... it's your life. YOUR life. Your LIFE.

:

:

:

:

:

:

:

:   **STOP DOING** ... freedom is your birthright

:

:

:

WANT TO CHANGE ... naming it is liberating   **GRATITUDE** ... expands your consciousness

Be done with enduring.

GRACIOUS

SATURDAY July 22 | 2017
Sun enters Leo

SUNDAY July 23 | 2017
● New Moon

THIS I WILL DO TO FEEL
THE WAY I WANT TO FEEL

TO-DO ... make choices that liberate you

TO-DO ... your desires are sacred

REFLECT ... this week I learned

ENVISION ... what do you *really* want to happen?

FUN

You know the answer.

MY CORE DESIRED FEELINGS

SOUL PROMPT ... three words that describe your anger

SCHEDULE ... simplicity is freedom

   :
   :
   :
   :
   :
   :
   :
   :
   :
   :
   :
   :
   :

3 THINGS ... get this done and the rest is a bonus

TO-DO ... keep your soul on the agenda

STOP DOING ... *No* makes way for *Yes*

WANT TO CHANGE ... claim it. Tame it.

GRATITUDE ... specificity intensifies gratitude

Even in your despair, you are magnificent.

LIGHT

MY CORE DESIRED FEELINGS

WHAT I WILL DO TO FEEL
THE WAY I WANT TO FEEL

SOUL PROMPT ... my power

SCHEDULE ... reframe "obligations" into "choices"

3 THINGS ... that are moving your life forward

TO-DO ... prioritize pleasure

STOP DOING ... work for Love

WANT TO CHANGE ... the solution will come

GRATITUDE ... note WHY you're grateful

GLAMOROUS

More gratitude = less resentment.

WHAT
THE WA

SOUL PROMPT ... I forgive

SCHEDULE ... does it light you up?

:
:
:
:
:
:
:
:
:
:
:
:
:
:

3 THINGS ... that are doable today

TO-DO ... less striving, more living

STOP DOING ... don't take any crap

WANT TO CHANGE ... clarity is power

GRATITUDE ... puts everything into perspective

Decide to just get over it. Let it be that simple.

FAITH

MY CORE DESIRED FEELINGS

WHAT I WILL DO TO FEEL
THE WAY I WANT TO FEEL

SOUL PROMPT ... my favourite feeling is

SCHEDULE ... respect yourself

:
:
:
:
:
:
:
:
:
:
:
:
:
:
:

3 THINGS ... that matter most

TO-DO ... the WHOLE point is to feel good

STOP DOING ... does it feel light or heavy?

WANT TO CHANGE ... why should it be different?

GRATITUDE ... challenges are teachers

ARTICULATE

Stand up for yourself. (Some people will take this personally. It's okay.)

MY CORE DESIRED FEELINGS

SOUL PROMPT ... what do you have to offer?

SCHEDULE ... joy expands time

:

:

:

:

:

:

:

:

:

:

:

:

:

:

3 THINGS ... because focus creates momentum

TO-DO ... it's your life. YOUR life. Your LIFE.

STOP DOING ... freedom is your birthright

WANT TO CHANGE ... naming it is liberating

GRATITUDE ... expands your consciousness

Let go of what's not working.

DEPTH

WHAT I WILL DO TO FEEL
THE WAY I WANT TO FEEL

TO-DO ... make choices that liberate you

TO-DO ... your desires are sacred

REFLECT ... what's true for you?

ENVISION ... let it be easy

BLESSED

Bliss. Anger. Gentleness. Grief. Desperation. Joy. Joy. Joy. All in one day.

MY CORE DESIRED FEELINGS

WHAT I WILL DO IN SEE
THE WAY I WANT TO FEEL

SOUL PROMPT ... no matter what

SCHEDULE ... simplicity is freedom

   :

   :

   :

   :

   :

   :

   :

   :

   :

   :

   :

   :

   :

   :

3 THINGS ... get this done and the rest is a bonus

TO-DO ... keep your soul on the agenda

STOP DOING ... *No makes way for Yes*

WANT TO CHANGE ... claim it. Tame it.

GRATITUDE ... specificity intensifies gratitude

COURAGE

You are a portal to the truth.

AUGUST
2017

adoring

alluring

amour

attractive

desirable

embodied

gorgeous

hot

impassioned

passion

passionate

sensing

sensual

sensuous

sexy

turned on

AUGUST

MONDAY	TUESDAY	WEDNESDAY
WEEK 31	**Lughnasadh** 1	2
O Full Moon Lunar Eclipse 7 WEEK 32	8	9
14 WEEK 33	15	16
● New Moon 21 Solar Eclipse WEEK 34	Sun enters Virgo 22	23
28 WEEK 35	29	30

THURSDAY	FRIDAY	SATURDAY	SUNDAY
3	4	5	6
10	11	12 Mercury goes retrograde	13
17	18	19	20
24	25	26	27
31			

AUGUST 2017 MONTHLY CHECK-IN

My Core Desired Feelings:

Feelings inform your wellness, your creations, your wisdom. Tune in to the predominant and new feelings that are running through you these days.

My major intentions & goals for the year:

Revisit your vision. When your core desired feelings lead the way, both your goals and how you go after them become more satisfying. How are your goals a reflection of how you most want to feel?

To generate my CDFs through my intentions & goals, I will:

What will it take to fulfill your vision for the year? Evaluate, affirm, or adjust your to-dos and intentions according to what you think will generate your core desired feelings along the way.

FINANCIALLY FREE

MY CORE DESIRED FEELINGS

SOUL PROMPT ... I Love that I'm so

SCHEDULE ... reframe "obligations" into "choices"

:
:
:
:
:
:
:
:
:
:
:
:
:
:
:

3 THINGS ... that are moving your life forward

TO-DO ... prioritize pleasure

STOP DOING ... work for Love

WANT TO CHANGE ... the solution will come

GRATITUDE ... note WHY you're grateful

SELF-NURTURED

Worship your vision.

MY CORE DESIRED FEELINGS

SOUL PROMPT ... two things you are doing to care for your body

SCHEDULE ... does it light you up?

:

:

:

:

:

:

:

:

:

:

:

:

:

3 THINGS ... that are doable today

TO-DO ... less striving, more living

STOP DOING ... don't take any crap

WANT TO CHANGE ... clarity is power

GRATITUDE ... puts everything into perspective

Unhook. Return the hook to where it came from.

PERSEVERANCE

MY CORE DESIRED FEELINGS

WHAT I WILL DO TO FEEL
THE WAY I WANT TO FEEL

SOUL PROMPT ... today, my heart feels

SCHEDULE ... respect yourself

3 THINGS ... that matter most

TO-DO ... the WHOLE point is to feel good

STOP DOING ... does it feel light or heavy?

WANT TO CHANGE ... why should it be different?

GRATITUDE ... challenges are teachers

WORTHY

Respect your wishes.

MY CORE DESIRED FEELINGS

WHAT WOULD LOVE DO? GET OUT OF THE WAY AND LET IT HAPPEN

SOUL PROMPT ... word for the day

SCHEDULE ... joy expands time

- :
- :
- :
- :
- :
- :
- :
- :
- :
- :
- :
- :
- :
- :

3 THINGS ... because focus creates momentum

TO-DO ... it's your life. YOUR life. Your LIFE.

STOP DOING ... freedom is your birthright

WANT TO CHANGE ... naming it is liberating

GRATITUDE ... expands your consciousness

Welcome confusion.

MINDFUL

TO-DO ... make choices that liberate you

TO-DO ... your desires are sacred

REFLECT ... speak up

ENVISION ... your soul is rooting for you

LUSH

Change the game.

MONDAY August 7 | 2017
○ Full Moon | Lunar Eclipse

MY CORE DESIRED FEELINGS

SOUL PROMPT ... I'm never

SCHEDULE ... simplicity is freedom

:

:

:

:

:

:

:

:

:

:

:

:

:

:

3 THINGS ... get this done and the rest is a bonus

TO-DO ... keep your soul on the agenda

STOP DOING ... *No* makes way for *Yes*

WANT TO CHANGE ... claim it. Tame it.

GRATITUDE ... specificity intensifies gratitude

You are the temple.

WHAT I WILL DO TO FEEL
THE WAY I WANT TO FEEL

SOUL PROMPT ... two things you're doing to clean up the past

SCHEDULE ... reframe "obligations" into "choices"

3 THINGS ... that are moving your life forward

TO-DO ... prioritize pleasure

STOP DOING ... work for Love

WANT TO CHANGE ... the solution will come

GRATITUDE ... note WHY you're grateful

GRITTY

Surprise your doubts with action.

WHAT I WILL DO TODAY & THE WAY I WANT TO FEEL

SOUL PROMPT ... I'm frightened of

SCHEDULE ... does it light you up?

- :
- :
- :
- :
- :
- :
- :
- :
- :
- :
- :
- :
- :
- :

3 THINGS ... that are doable today

TO-DO ... less striving, more living

STOP DOING ... don't take any crap

WANT TO CHANGE ... clarity is power

GRATITUDE ... puts everything into perspective

Love is always happy to see you.

STRONG

MY CORE DESIRED FEELINGS

SOUL PROMPT ... today, my heart feels

SCHEDULE ... respect yourself

:
:
:
:
:
:
:
:
:
:
:
:
:

3 THINGS ... that matter most

TO-DO ... the WHOLE point is to feel good

STOP DOING ... does it feel light or heavy?

WANT TO CHANGE ... why should it be different?

GRATITUDE ... challenges are teachers

PASSION

Comparison is a slippery slope to jealousy.

MY CORE DESIRED FEELINGS

SOUL PROMPT ... what are the opposite feelings of how you want to feel?

SCHEDULE ... joy expands time

- :
- :
- :
- :
- :
- :
- :
- :
- :
- :
- :
- :
- :
- :

3 THINGS ... because focus creates momentum

TO-DO ... it's your life. YOUR life. Your LIFE.

STOP DOING ... freedom is your birthright

WANT TO CHANGE ... naming it is liberating

GRATITUDE ... expands your consciousness

Grace is the cousin of synchronicity.

TENDER

WHAT I WILL DO TO FEEL
THE WAY I WANT TO FEEL

TO-DO ... make choices that liberate you

TO-DO ... your desires are sacred

REFLECT ... enthusiasm saves lives

ENVISION ... I'm devoted to

DELIGHT

The universe cannot resist authenticity.

WHAT I LOVE
THE MOST

SOUL PROMPT ... I'm growing

SCHEDULE ... simplicity is freedom

:
:
:
:
:
:
:
:
:
:
:
:
:
:

3 THINGS ... get this done and the rest is a bonus

TO-DO ... keep your soul on the agenda

STOP DOING ... *No* makes way for *Yes*

WANT TO CHANGE ... claim it. Tame it.

GRATITUDE ... specificity intensifies gratitude

Are you willing to change?

LOVING

WHAT I WILL DO TO FEEL
THE WAY I WANT TO FEEL

SOUL PROMPT ... one word to describe your work in the world

SCHEDULE ... reframe "obligations" into "choices"

:
:
:
:
:
:
:
:
:
:
:
:
:
:

3 THINGS ... that are moving your life forward

TO-DO ... prioritize pleasure

STOP DOING ... work for Love

WANT TO CHANGE ... the solution will come

GRATITUDE ... note WHY you're grateful

EXPLORER

It's possible.

SOUL PROMPT ... I'm giving up

SCHEDULE ... does it light you up?

- :
- :
- :
- :
- :
- :
- :
- :
- :
- :
- :
- :
- :
- :

3 THINGS ... that are doable today

TO-DO ... less striving, more living

STOP DOING ... don't take any crap

WANT TO CHANGE ... clarity is power

GRATITUDE ... puts everything into perspective

devotion cures

ORGANIZED

MY CORE DESIRED FEELINGS

WHAT I WILL DO TO FEEL
THE WAY I WANT TO FEEL

SOUL PROMPT ... today, my heart feels

SCHEDULE ... respect yourself

:
:
:
:
:
:
:
:
:
:
:
:
:
:

3 THINGS ... that matter most

TO-DO ... the WHOLE point is to feel good

STOP DOING ... does it feel light or heavy?

WANT TO CHANGE ... why should it be different?

GRATITUDE ... challenges are teachers

AMBITIOUS

Want what you want with all your heart.

MY CORE DESIRED FEELINGS

WHAT
THE

SOUL PROMPT ... I want space to

SCHEDULE ... joy expands time

:
:
:
:
:
:
:
:
:
:
:
:
:
:

3 THINGS ... because focus creates momentum

TO-DO ... it's your life. YOUR life. Your LIFE.

STOP DOING ... freedom is your birthright

WANT TO CHANGE ... naming it is liberating

GRATITUDE ... expands your consciousness

You'll do it when you're ready.

KINDRED

TODAY I WILL DO TO FEEL
THE WAY I WANT TO FEEL

TO-DO ... make choices that liberate you

TO-DO ... your desires are sacred

REFLECT ... rest

ENVISION ... don't hold back

CHARMED

Declare your intentions.

MY CORE DESIRED FEELINGS

SOUL PROMPT Less . . . . would be good.

SCHEDULE ... simplicity is freedom

:

:

:

:

:

:

:

:

:

:

:

:

:

:

WANT TO CHANGE ... claim it. Tame it.

3 THINGS ... get this done and the rest is a bonus

TO-DO ... keep your soul on the agenda

STOP DOING ... *No makes way for Yes*

GRATITUDE ... specificity intensifies gratitude

A prayer: may my suffering be of service.

MIRACULOUS

MY CORE DESIRED FEELINGS

WHAT I WILL DO TO FEEL
THE WAY I WANT TO FEEL

SOUL PROMPT ... I notice

SCHEDULE ... reframe "obligations" into "choices"

:
:
:
:
:
:
:
:
:
:
:
:
:
:

3 THINGS ... that are moving your life forward

TO-DO ... prioritize pleasure

STOP DOING ... work for Love

WANT TO CHANGE ... the solution will come

GRATITUDE ... note WHY you're grateful

HAPPY

Use the intelligence of your heart

W H A T
T H E

SOUL PROMPT ... who is most helpful in your career right now?

SCHEDULE ... does it light you up?

- :
- :
- :
- :
- :
- :
- :
- :
- :
- :
- :
- :
- :
- :

3 THINGS ... that are doable today

TO-DO ... less striving, more living

STOP DOING ... don't take any crap

WANT TO CHANGE ... clarity is power

GRATITUDE ... puts everything into perspective

Greet your pain. It brings gifts.

SELF-SUFFICIENT

MY CORE DESIRED FEELINGS

WHAT I WILL DO TO FEEL
THE WAY I WANT TO FEEL

SOUL PROMPT ... today, my heart feels

SCHEDULE ... respect yourself

:
:
:
:
:
:
:
:
:
:
:
:
:

3 THINGS ... that matter most

TO-DO ... the WHOLE point is to feel good

STOP DOING ... does it feel light or heavy?

WANT TO CHANGE ... why should it be different?

GRATITUDE ... challenges are teachers

LIBERATED

Honour what's primal.

SOUL PROMPT ... I regret

SCHEDULE ... joy expands time

:
:
:
:
:
:
:
:
:
:
:
:
:
:

3 THINGS ... because focus creates momentum

TO-DO ... it's your life. YOUR life. Your LIFE.

STOP DOING ... freedom is your birthright

WANT TO CHANGE ... naming it is liberating

GRATITUDE ... expands your consciousness

Rinse off your resentments.

ROOTED

WHAT I WILL DO TO FEEL
THE WAY I WANT TO FEEL

TO-DO ... make choices that liberate you

TO-DO ... your desires are sacred

REFLECT ... this week I learned

ENVISION ... what do you *really* want to happen?

ILLUMINABLE

Fantasize.

WHAT
THE WAY

SOUL PROMPT . . . . melts me.

SCHEDULE ... simplicity is freedom

:

:

:

:

:

:

:

:

:

:

:

:

:

:

3 THINGS ... get this done and the rest is a bonus

TO-DO ... keep your soul on the agenda

STOP DOING ... *No* makes way for *Yes*

WANT TO CHANGE ... claim it. Tame it.

GRATITUDE ... specificity intensifies gratitude

Romance the future.

UNITED

MY CORE DESIRED FEELINGS

WHAT I WILL DO TO FEEL
THE WAY I WANT TO FEEL

SOUL PROMPT ... I am here to

SCHEDULE ... reframe "obligations" into "choices"

:
:
:
:
:
:
:
:
:
:
:
:
:
:

3 THINGS ... that are moving your life forward

TO-DO ... prioritize pleasure

STOP DOING ... work for Love

WANT TO CHANGE ... the solution will come

GRATITUDE ... note WHY you're grateful

TOGETHER

Joy is an indicator of deep wellness.

SOUL PROMPT ... what do people thank you for the most?

SCHEDULE ... does it light you up?

:

:

:

:

:

:

:

:

:

:

:

:

:

:

3 THINGS ... that are doable today

TO-DO ... less striving, more living

STOP DOING ... don't take any crap

WANT TO CHANGE ... clarity is power

GRATITUDE ... puts everything into perspective

Teach them how to Love.

DYNAMIC

WHAT I WILL DO TO FEEL
THE WAY I WANT TO FEEL

SOUL PROMPT ... today, my heart feels

SCHEDULE ... respect yourself

3 THINGS ... that matter most

TO-DO ... the WHOLE point is to feel good

STOP DOING ... does it feel light or heavy?

WANT TO CHANGE ... why should it be different?

GRATITUDE ... challenges are teachers

VIVACIOUS

You're having an effect.

IDEAS. DESIRES. WISDOM. ... feel free

Change your questions, change your life.

SUPPORTED

SEPTEMBER
2017

accomplished
determination
determined
effective
effectual
focused
grounded
grounding
mindful
momentum
positive
productive
purposeful
security
serving

MONDAY	TUESDAY	WEDNESDAY
WEEK 35		
Labour Day 4	Mercury turns direct 5	O Full Moon 6
WEEK 36		
11	12	13
WEEK 37		
18	19	● New Moon 20
WEEK 38		
Family & Community Day (AUS) 25	26	27
WEEK 39		

THURSDAY	FRIDAY	SATURDAY	SUNDAY
	1	2	3
7	8	9	10
14	15	16	17
21	**Autumn Equinox/ Mabon** Sun enters Libra 22	23	24
28	29	30	

SEPTEMBER

SEPTEMBER 2017 MONTHLY CHECK-IN

My Core Desired Feelings:

Feelings inform your wellness, your creations, your wisdom. Tune in to the predominant
and new feelings that are running through you these days.

My major intentions & goals for the year:

Revisit your vision. When your core desired feelings lead the way, both your goals and how you go
after them become more satisfying. How are your goals a reflection of how you most want to feel?

To generate my CDFs through my intentions & goals, I will:

What will it take to fulfill your vision for the year? Evaluate, affirm, or adjust your to-dos and
intentions according to what you think will generate your core desired feelings along the way.

LUXURIOUS

IDEAS. DESIRES. WISDOM. ... take up space

REAL

WHAT I WILL DO TO FEEL
THE WAY I WANT TO FEEL

SOUL PROMPT ... I declare that my life purpose is

SCHEDULE ... joy expands time

3 THINGS ... because focus creates momentum

TO-DO ... it's your life. YOUR life. Your LIFE.

STOP DOING ... freedom is your birthright

WANT TO CHANGE ... naming it is liberating

GRATITUDE ... expands your consciousness

ESSENTIAL

Focus on healing.

TO-DO ... make choices that liberate you

TO-DO ... your desires are sacred

REFLECT ... what's true for you?

ENVISION ... let it be easy

You're in.

MY CORE DESIRED FEELINGS

WHAT I WILL DO TO FEEL
THE WAY I WANT TO FEEL

SOUL PROMPT ... how is your heart today?

SCHEDULE ... simplicity is freedom

3 THINGS ... get this done and the rest is a bonus

TO-DO ... keep your soul on the agenda

STOP DOING ... *No* makes way for *Yes*

WANT TO CHANGE ... claim it. Tame it.

GRATITUDE ... specificity intensifies gratitude

FREE-FLOWING

The universe Loves a believer.

SOUL PROMPT ... what do you need to let go of this week?

SCHEDULE ... reframe "obligations" into "choices"

- :
- :
- :
- :
- :
- :
- :
- :
- :
- :
- :
- :
- :
- :

3 THINGS ... that are moving your life forward

TO-DO ... prioritize pleasure

STOP DOING ... work for Love

WANT TO CHANGE ... the solution will come

GRATITUDE ... note WHY you're grateful

Peace of mind is power.

INFLUENTIAL

MY CORE DESIRED FEELINGS

WHAT I WILL DO TO FEEL
THE WAY I WANT TO FEEL

SOUL PROMPT ... your greatest desire in terms of your livelihood

SCHEDULE ... does it light you up?

3 THINGS ... that are doable today

TO-DO ... less striving, more living

STOP DOING ... don't take any crap

WANT TO CHANGE ... clarity is power

GRATITUDE ... puts everything into perspective

BLOOMING

Your self-expression is a great service to the world.

WHAT
THE

SOUL PROMPT ... today, my heart feels

SCHEDULE ... respect yourself

:
:
:
:
:
:
:
:
:
:
:
:
:
:

3 THINGS ... that matter most

TO-DO ... the WHOLE point is to feel good

STOP DOING ... does it feel light or heavy?

WANT TO CHANGE ... why should it be different?

GRATITUDE ... challenges are teachers

What's driving your self-improvement?

GROOVIN'

WHAT I WILL DO TO FEEL
THE WAY I WANT TO FEEL

SOUL PROMPT I need to talk to . . . . about . . . .

SCHEDULE ... joy expands time

:
:
:
:
:
:
:
:
:
:
:
:
:
:

3 THINGS ... because focus creates momentum

TO-DO ... it's your life. YOUR life. Your LIFE.

STOP DOING ... freedom is your birthright

WANT TO CHANGE ... naming it is liberating

GRATITUDE ... expands your consciousness

CHERISHMENT

Take the help.

WHAT I WILL DO TO FEEL THE WAY I WANT TO FEEL

SOUL PROMPT ... I'm super anticipating

SCHEDULE ... simplicity is freedom

3 THINGS ... get this done and the rest is a bonus

TO-DO ... keep your soul on the agenda

STOP DOING ... *No* makes way for *Yes*

WANT TO CHANGE ... claim it. Tame it.

GRATITUDE ... specificity intensifies gratitude

SOULFUL CLARITY

Positive feelings are a form of power.

WHAT I WILL DO TO FEEL
THE WAY I WANT TO FEEL

TO-DO ... make choices that liberate you

. . . .

. . . .

. . . .

. . . .

. . . .

REFLECT ... speak up

TO-DO ... your desires are sacred

. . . .

. . . .

. . . .

. . . .

. . . .

ENVISION ... your soul is rooting for you

Give it all you got, and then let it go.

FULFILLED

MY CORE DESIRED FEELINGS

WHAT I WILL DO TO FEEL
THE WAY I WANT TO FEEL

SOUL PROMPT ... where are you headed?

SCHEDULE ... reframe "obligations" into "choices"

:
:
:
:
:
:
:
:
:
:
:
:
:
:

3 THINGS ... that are moving your life forward

TO-DO ... prioritize pleasure

STOP DOING ... work for Love

WANT TO CHANGE ... the solution will come

GRATITUDE ... note WHY you're grateful

Exercise your right to negotiate.

HARMONIOUS

WHAT I WILL DO TO FEEL
THE WAY I WANT TO FEEL

SOUL PROMPT ... I want to learn

SCHEDULE ... does it light you up?

: . . . .
: . . . .
: . . . .
: . . . .
: . . . .
: . . . .
: . . . .
: . . . .
: . . . .
: . . . .
: . . . .
: . . . .
: . . . .

3 THINGS ... that are doable today

TO-DO ... less striving, more living

STOP DOING ... don't take any crap

WANT TO CHANGE ... clarity is power

GRATITUDE ... puts everything into perspective

VISIONARY

your body is a miracle

WHAT I WILL DO TO FEEL
THE WAY I WANT TO FEEL

SOUL PROMPT ... today, my heart feels

SCHEDULE ... respect yourself

:
:
:
:
:
:
:
:
:
:
:
:
:

3 THINGS ... that matter most

TO-DO ... the WHOLE point is to feel good

STOP DOING ... does it feel light or heavy?

WANT TO CHANGE ... why should it be different?

GRATITUDE ... challenges are teachers

Love what you see.

INTIMATE

MY CORE DESIRED FEELINGS

WHAT I WILL DO TO FEEL
THE WAY I WANT TO FEEL

SOUL PROMPT ... what can you give away?

SCHEDULE ... joy expands time

3 THINGS ... because focus creates momentum

:

:

:

:

TO-DO ... it's your life. YOUR life. Your LIFE.

:

:

:

:

:

:

STOP DOING ... freedom is your birthright

:

:

:

WANT TO CHANGE ... naming it is liberating

GRATITUDE ... expands your consciousness

INCREDIBLE

You will fail. Eventually. Whatever.

WHAT I WILL DO TO FEEL
THE WAY I WANT TO FEEL

TO-DO ... make choices that liberate you

TO-DO ... your desires are sacred

REFLECT ... enthusiasm saves lives

ENVISION ... I'm devoted to

Let pleasure distract you.

GIDDY

MY CORE DESIRED FEELINGS

WHAT I WILL DO TO FEEL
THE WAY I WANT TO FEEL

SOUL PROMPT ... what do you need to create space for?

SCHEDULE ... simplicity is freedom

3 THINGS ... get this done and the rest is a bonus

TO-DO ... keep your soul on the agenda

STOP DOING ... *No* makes way for *Yes*

WANT TO CHANGE ... claim it. Tame it.

GRATITUDE ... specificity intensifies gratitude

Your muse LOVES to be appreciated.

MOTIVATIONAL

MY CORE DESIRED FEELINGS

WHAT I WILL DO TO FEEL
THE WAY I WANT TO FEEL

SOUL PROMPT ... what are you building?

SCHEDULE ... reframe "obligations" into "choices"

:
:
:
:
:
:
:
:
:
:
:
:
:
:

3 THINGS ... that are moving your life forward

TO-DO ... prioritize pleasure

STOP DOING ... work for Love

WANT TO CHANGE ... the solution will come

GRATITUDE ... note WHY you're grateful

Seriously, it does NOT MATTER what they think.

IN AWE

MY CORE DESIRED FEELINGS

WHAT I WILL DO TO FEEL THE WAY I WANT TO FEEL

SOUL PROMPT ... where can you go for inspiration?

SCHEDULE ... does it light you up?

:
:
:
:
:
:
:
:
:
:
:
:
:
:

3 THINGS ... that are doable today

TO-DO ... less striving, more living

STOP DOING ... don't take any crap

WANT TO CHANGE ... clarity is power

GRATITUDE ... puts everything into perspective

MAGNIFICENT

Want to bring out the best in people? Ask them how they want to feel.

WHAT I WILL DO TO FEEL
THE WAY I WANT TO FEEL

SOUL PROMPT ... today, my heart feels

SCHEDULE ... respect yourself

3 THINGS ... that matter most

TO-DO ... the WHOLE point is to feel good

STOP DOING ... does it feel light or heavy?

WANT TO CHANGE ... why should it be different?

GRATITUDE ... challenges are teachers

Believe what you want.

POTENT

Autumn Equinox/Mabon
Sun enters Libra

WHAT I WILL DO TO FEEL
THE WAY I WANT TO FEEL

SOUL PROMPT ... where or how do you need to stop over-giving?

SCHEDULE ... joy expands time

:
:
:
:
:
:
:
:
:
:
:
:
:
:

3 THINGS ... because focus creates momentum

TO-DO ... it's your life. YOUR life. Your LIFE.

STOP DOING ... freedom is your birthright

WANT TO CHANGE ... naming it is liberating

GRATITUDE ... expands your consciousness

EMERGENT

Take back what's yours.

WHAT I WILL DO TO FEEL THE WAY I WANT TO FEEL

TO-DO ... make choices that liberate you

....

....

....

....

....

REFLECT ... rest

TO-DO ... your desires are sacred

....

....

....

....

ENVISION ... don't hold back

Selectively Love everyone.

SPACIOUS

MY CORE DESIRED FEELINGS

WHAT I WILL DO TO FEEL
THE WAY I WANT TO FEEL

SOUL PROMPT ... what relationship needs the most healing?

SCHEDULE ... simplicity is freedom

3 THINGS ... get this done and the rest is a bonus

TO-DO ... keep your soul on the agenda

STOP DOING ... *No* makes way for *Yes*

WANT TO CHANGE ... claim it. Tame it.

GRATITUDE ... specificity intensifies gratitude

BEAUTY

True desires come with the capacity to be fulfilled.

MY CORE DESIRED FEELINGS

WHAT I WILL DO TO FEEL
THE WAY I WANT TO FEEL

SOUL PROMPT ... I want to be known for

SCHEDULE ... reframe "obligations" into "choices"

:
:
:
:
:
:
:
:
:
:
:
:
:
:

3 THINGS ... that are moving your life forward

TO-DO ... prioritize pleasure

STOP DOING ... work for Love

WANT TO CHANGE ... the solution will come

GRATITUDE ... note WHY you're grateful

Only make high-vibration commitments.

LIT UP

WHAT I WILL DO TO FEEL THE WAY I WANT TO FEEL

SOUL PROMPT ... how can you be encouraging today?

SCHEDULE ... does it light you up?

:
:
:
:
:
:
:
:
:
:
:
:
:
:

3 THINGS ... that are doable today

TO-DO ... less striving, more living

STOP DOING ... don't take any crap

WANT TO CHANGE ... clarity is power

GRATITUDE ... puts everything into perspective

GROUNDED

Happiness returns more quickly when you give yourself permission to be blue.

MY CORE DESIRED FEELINGS

WHAT I WILL DO TO FEEL
THE WAY I WANT TO FEEL

SOUL PROMPT ... today, my heart feels

SCHEDULE ... respect yourself

:
:
:
:
:
:
:
:
:
:
:
:
:

3 THINGS ... that matter most

TO-DO ... the WHOLE point is to feel good

STOP DOING ... does it feel light or heavy?

WANT TO CHANGE ... why should it be different?

GRATITUDE ... challenges are teachers

Only you need to trust your intuition.

ALIGNED

WHAT I WILL DO TO FEEL THE WAY I WANT TO FEEL

SOUL PROMPT ... most recent compliment I received

SCHEDULE ... joy expands time

3 THINGS ... because focus creates momentum

TO-DO ... it's your life. YOUR life. Your LIFE.

STOP DOING ... freedom is your birthright

WANT TO CHANGE ... naming it is liberating

GRATITUDE ... expands your consciousness

READY

Turn your longing into a calling.

WHAT I WILL DO TO FEEL THE WAY I WANT TO FEEL

TO-DO ... make choices that liberate you

....

....

....

....

....

REFLECT ... this week I learned

Safety is only a habit.

BOLDLY COURAGEOUS

OCTOBER
2017

abundance
abundant
blessed
blessings
fortunate
generosity
generous
grateful
gratitude
opulent
opulence
plentiful
prosperity
prosperous
thankful
treasure

OCTOBER

MONDAY	TUESDAY	WEDNESDAY
WEEK 39		
Labour Day (AUS) 2	3	4
WEEK 40		
Columbus Day (US) 9 **Thanksgiving (CAN)**	10	11
WEEK 41		
16	17	18
WEEK 42		
Diwali ends 23 Sun enters Scorpio	24	25
WEEK 43		
Yom Kippur ends 30 **(evening)**	**Halloween/** 31 **Samhain**	
WEEK 44		

THURSDAY	FRIDAY	SATURDAY	SUNDAY
			1
O Full Moon 5	6	7	8
12	13	14	15
Diwali begins 19 ● New Moon	**Rosh Hashanah begins (evening)** 20	21	**Rosh Hashanah ends (evening)** 22
26	27	28	**Yom Kippur begins (evening)** 29

OCTOBER 2017 MONTHLY CHECK-IN

My Core Desired Feelings:

Feelings inform your wellness, your creations, your wisdom. Tune in to the predominant
and new feelings that are running through you these days.

My major intentions & goals for the year:

Revisit your vision. When your core desired feelings lead the way, both your goals and how you go
after them become more satisfying. How are your goals a reflection of how you most want to feel?

To generate my CDFs through my intentions & goals, I will:

What will it take to fulfill your vision for the year? Evaluate, affirm, or adjust your to-dos and
intentions according to what you think will generate your core desired feelings along the way.

INSPIRATIONAL

IDEAS. DESIRES. WISDOM. ... your heart is genius

HELPFUL

WHAT I WILL DO TO FEEL
THE WAY I WANT TO FEEL

TO-DO ... your desires are sacred

. . . .

. . . .

. . . .

. . . .

. . . .

ENVISION ... what do you *really* want to happen?

ARDENT

Question your sanity.

WHAT I WILL DO TO FEEL
THE WAY I WANT TO FEEL

SOUL PROMPT ... I want to give more

SCHEDULE ... simplicity is freedom

: ....
: ....
: ....
: ....
: ....
: ....
: ....
: ....
: ....
: ....
: ....
: ....
: ....
: ....

3 THINGS ... get this done and the rest is a bonus

....
....
....

TO-DO ... keep your soul on the agenda

....
....
....
....
....

STOP DOING ... *No* makes way for *Yes*

WANT TO CHANGE ... claim it. Tame it.

GRATITUDE ... specificity intensifies gratitude

Try staying open when you want to shut down. It changes everything.

ZOETIC

MY CORE DESIRED FEELINGS

WHAT I WILL DO TO FEEL
THE WAY I WANT TO FEEL

SOUL PROMPT ... I'm done with

SCHEDULE ... reframe "obligations" into "choices"

:
:
:
:
:
:
:
:
:
:
:
:
:

3 THINGS ... that are moving your life forward

TO-DO ... prioritize pleasure

STOP DOING ... work for Love

WANT TO CHANGE ... the solution will come

GRATITUDE ... note WHY you're grateful

HOLISTIC

Risk being misunderstood. It's usually worth it.

MY CORE DESIRED FEELINGS

WHAT I WILL DO TO FEEL
THE WAY I WANT TO FEEL

SOUL PROMPT ... today, my heart feels

SCHEDULE ... does it light you up?

: ....
: ....
: ....
: ....
: ....
: ....
: ....
: ....
: ....
: ....
: ....
: ....
: ....
: ....

3 THINGS ... that are doable today

TO-DO ... less striving, more living

STOP DOING ... don't take any crap

WANT TO CHANGE ... clarity is power

GRATITUDE ... puts everything into perspective

Embrace the intensity.

FULL

THURSDAY October 5 | 2017
O Full Moon

MY CORE DESIRED FEELINGS

WHAT I WILL DO TO FEEL
THE WAY I WANT TO FEEL

SOUL PROMPT ... three reasons you are an incredible individual

SCHEDULE ... respect yourself

3 THINGS ... that matter most

TO-DO ... the WHOLE point is to feel good

STOP DOING ... does it feel light or heavy?

WANT TO CHANGE ... why should it be different?

GRATITUDE ... challenges are teachers

BLAZING

Seeing the futility is so liberating.

MY CORE DESIRED FEELINGS

WHAT I WILL DO TO FEEL THE WAY I WANT TO FEEL

SOUL PROMPT ... what do you wish you had courage for?

SCHEDULE ... joy expands time

  :
  :
  :
  :
  :
  :
  :
  :
  :
  :
  :
  :
  :
  :

3 THINGS ... because focus creates momentum

TO-DO ... it's your life. YOUR life. Your LIFE.

STOP DOING ... freedom is your birthright

WANT TO CHANGE ... naming it is liberating

GRATITUDE ... expands your consciousness

Leave the flock.

IGNITED

WHAT I WILL DO TO FEEL THE WAY I WANT TO FEEL

TO-DO ... make choices that liberate you

....

....

....

....

....

REFLECT ... what's true for you?

TO-DO ... your desires are sacred

....

....

....

....

....

ENVISION ... let it be easy

CELEBRATED

If you want the best out of life, it requires the best of you.

MONDAY October 9 | 2017

Columbus Day (US) | Thanksgiving (CAN)

WHAT I WILL DO TO FEEL
THE WAY I WANT TO FEEL

SOUL PROMPT ... I rely on

SCHEDULE ... simplicity is freedom

: ....
: ....
: ....
: ....
: ....
: ....
: ....
: ....
: ....
: ....
: ....
: ....
: ....
: ....

3 THINGS ... get this done and the rest is a bonus

TO-DO ... keep your soul on the agenda

STOP DOING ... *No* makes way for *Yes*

WANT TO CHANGE ... claim it. Tame it.

GRATITUDE ... specificity intensifies gratitude

"'Cause I wanna" is a good enough reason.

SHINING

WHAT I WILL DO TO FEEL THE WAY I WANT TO FEEL

SOUL PROMPT ... most favourite recent insight

SCHEDULE ... reframe "obligations" into "choices"

: ....
: ....
: ....
: ....
: ....
: ....
: ....
: ....
: ....
: ....
: ....
: ....
: ....

3 THINGS ... that are moving your life forward

....
....
....

TO-DO ... prioritize pleasure

....
....
....
....
....

STOP DOING ... work for Love

WANT TO CHANGE ... the solution will come

GRATITUDE ... note WHY you're grateful

ECSTACY

Over-controlling will make you brittle.

WHAT I WILL DO TO FEEL
THE WAY I WANT TO FEEL

SOUL PROMPT ... today, my heart feels

SCHEDULE ... does it light you up?

3 THINGS ... that are doable today

TO-DO ... less striving, more living

STOP DOING ... don't take any crap

WANT TO CHANGE ... clarity is power

GRATITUDE ... puts everything into perspective

RELEASED

The easy way = more time to enjoy what you've got, and to get more of what you want.

MY CORE DESIRED FEELINGS

WHAT I WILL DO TO FEEL
THE WAY I WANT TO FEEL

SOUL PROMPT ... how do you feel about where you come from?

SCHEDULE ... respect yourself

- :
- :
- :
- :
- :
- :
- :
- :
- :
- :
- :
- :
- :

3 THINGS ... that matter most

TO-DO ... the WHOLE point is to feel good

STOP DOING ... does it feel light or heavy?

WANT TO CHANGE ... why should it be different?

GRATITUDE ... challenges are teachers

DIVINE FEMININITY

Change often triggers guilt.

MY CORE DESIRED FEELINGS

WHAT I WILL DO TO FEEL
THE WAY I WANT TO FEEL

SOUL PROMPT ... who do you want to know better?

SCHEDULE ... joy expands time

- :
- :
- :
- :
- :
- :
- :
- :
- :
- :
- :
- :
- :
- :

3 THINGS ... because focus creates momentum

TO-DO ... it's your life. YOUR life. Your LIFE.

STOP DOING ... freedom is your birthright

WANT TO CHANGE ... naming it is liberating

GRATITUDE ... expands your consciousness

APPRECIATED

Your pleasure enlightens other people.

WHAT I WILL DO TO FEEL
THE WAY I WANT TO FEEL

TO-DO ... make choices that liberate you

. . . .

. . . .

. . . .

. . . .

REFLECT ... speak up

TO-DO ... your desires are sacred

. . . .

. . . .

. . . .

. . . .

ENVISION ... your soul is rooting for you

ENCHANTMENT

find your tribe. love them hard.

WHAT I WILL DO TO FEEL THE WAY I WANT TO FEEL

SOUL PROMPT ... three encouraging things

SCHEDULE ... simplicity is freedom

: ....
: ....
: ....
: ....
: ....
: ....
: ....
: ....
: ....
: ....
: ....
: ....
: ....
: ....

3 THINGS ... get this done and the rest is a bonus

TO-DO ... keep your soul on the agenda

STOP DOING ... *No* makes way for *Yes*

WANT TO CHANGE ... claim it. Tame it.

GRATITUDE ... specificity intensifies gratitude

You are fucking glorious.

BLISSED OUT

MY CORE DESIRED FEELINGS

WHAT I WILL DO TO FEEL
THE WAY I WANT TO FEEL

SOUL PROMPT ... my energy is

SCHEDULE ... reframe "obligations" into "choices"

3 THINGS ... that are moving your life forward

- :
- :
- :
- :
- :
- :
- :
- :
- :
- :
- :
- :
- :

TO-DO ... prioritize pleasure

STOP DOING ... work for Love

WANT TO CHANGE ... the solution will come

GRATITUDE ... note WHY you're grateful

COMMUNITY

Fearlessness is a fat myth.

MY CORE DESIRED FEELINGS

WHAT I WILL DO TO FEEL
THE WAY I WANT TO FEEL

SOUL PROMPT ... today, my heart feels

SCHEDULE ... does it light you up?

- :
- :
- :
- :
- :
- :
- :
- :
- :
- :
- :
- :
- :
- :

3 THINGS ... that are doable today

TO-DO ... less striving, more living

STOP DOING ... don't take any crap

WANT TO CHANGE ... clarity is power

GRATITUDE ... puts everything into perspective

After logic...meditate.

OCEANIC

THURSDAY October 19 | 2017

Diwali begins
● New Moon

WHAT I WILL DO TO FEEL
THE WAY I WANT TO FEEL

SOUL PROMPT ... one word to describe my current struggle

SCHEDULE ... respect yourself

: ....
: ....
: ....
: ....
: ....
: ....
: ....
: ....
: ....
: ....
: ....
: ....
: ....
: ....

3 THINGS ... that matter most

....
....

TO-DO ... the WHOLE point is to feel good

....
....
....
....
....

STOP DOING ... does it feel light or heavy?

WANT TO CHANGE ... why should it be different?

GRATITUDE ... challenges are teachers

DEEPLY ROOTED

Seek passionately.

Rosh Hashanah begins (evening)

MY CORE DESIRED FEELINGS

WHAT I WILL DO TO FEEL
THE WAY I WANT TO FEEL

SOUL PROMPT ... my greatest strength is

SCHEDULE ... joy expands time

:
:
:
:
:
:
:
:
:
:
:
:
:
:

3 THINGS ... because focus creates momentum

TO-DO ... it's your life. YOUR life. Your LIFE.

STOP DOING ... freedom is your birthright

WANT TO CHANGE ... naming it is liberating

GRATITUDE ... expands your consciousness

Gravitate toward happiness.

SAFE

WHAT I WILL DO TO FEEL
THE WAY I WANT TO FEEL

TO-DO ... make choices that liberate you

. . . .

. . . .

. . . .

. . . .

. . . .

TO-DO ... your desires are sacred

. . . .

. . . .

. . . .

. . . .

. . . .

REFLECT ... enthusiasm saves lives

ENVISION ... I'm devoted to

ELEVATED

Think of suffering as self-compassion school.

Diwali ends
Sun enters Scorpio

MY CORE DESIRED FEELINGS

WHAT I WILL DO TO FEEL
THE WAY I WANT TO FEEL

SOUL PROMPT ... I'm stoked

SCHEDULE ... simplicity is freedom

:

:

:

:

:

:

:

:

:

:

:

:

:

:

3 THINGS ... get this done and the rest is a bonus

TO-DO ... keep your soul on the agenda

STOP DOING ... *No* makes way for *Yes*

WANT TO CHANGE ... claim it. Tame it.

GRATITUDE ... specificity intensifies gratitude

Strategy: start with Love.

TRIBAL

MY CORE DESIRED FEELINGS

WHAT I WILL DO TO FEEL
THE WAY I WANT TO FEEL

SOUL PROMPT ... if I were to start a charity it would be

SCHEDULE ... reframe "obligations" into "choices"

:

:

:

:

:

:

:

:

:

:

:

:

:

3 THINGS ... that are moving your life forward

TO-DO ... prioritize pleasure

STOP DOING ... work for Love

WANT TO CHANGE ... the solution will come

GRATITUDE ... note WHY you're grateful

FEARLESS

But do you feel free?

MY CORE DESIRED FEELINGS

WHAT I WILL DO TO FEEL
THE WAY I WANT TO FEEL

SOUL PROMPT ... today, my heart feels

SCHEDULE ... does it light you up?

:
:
:
:
:
:
:
:
:
:
:
:
:
:

3 THINGS ... that are doable today

TO-DO ... less striving, more living

STOP DOING ... don't take any crap

WANT TO CHANGE ... clarity is power

GRATITUDE ... puts everything into perspective

Freedom does not come from a checklist.

TURNED ON

MY CORE DESIRED FEELINGS

WHAT I WILL DO TO FEEL
THE WAY I WANT TO FEEL

SOUL PROMPT ... I'm all for

SCHEDULE ... respect yourself

3 THINGS ... that matter most

TO-DO ... the WHOLE point is to feel good

STOP DOING ... does it feel light or heavy?

WANT TO CHANGE ... why should it be different?

GRATITUDE ... challenges are teachers

NIRVANA

Do you want to be generally liked, or deeply adored?

MY CORE DESIRED FEELINGS

WHAT I WILL DO TO FEEL
THE WAY I WANT TO FEEL

SOUL PROMPT ... I'm curious about

SCHEDULE ... joy expands time

:
:
:
:
:
:
:
:
:
:
:
:
:
:

3 THINGS ... because focus creates momentum

TO-DO ... it's your life. YOUR life. Your LIFE.

STOP DOING ... freedom is your birthright

WANT TO CHANGE ... naming it is liberating

GRATITUDE ... expands your consciousness

If it doesn't feel good, STOP.

FEMININE

WHAT I WILL DO TO FEEL
THE WAY I WANT TO FEEL

TO-DO ... make choices that liberate you

....

....

....

....

....

REFLECT ... rest

TO-DO ... your desires are sacred

....

....

....

....

....

ENVISION ... don't hold back

ON PURPOSE

Root into your longing.

MONDAY October 30 | 2017
Yom Kippur ends (evening)

WHAT I WILL DO TO FEEL
THE WAY I WANT TO FEEL

SOUL PROMPT ... I identify with

SCHEDULE ... simplicity is freedom

:
:
:
:
:
:
:
:
:
:
:
:
:
:

3 THINGS ... get this done and the rest is a bonus

TO-DO ... keep your soul on the agenda

STOP DOING ... *No* makes way for *Yes*

WANT TO CHANGE ... claim it. Tame it.

GRATITUDE ... specificity intensifies gratitude

Leave room for magic.

ENERGETIC

MY CORE DESIRED FEELINGS

WHAT I WILL DO TO FEEL THE WAY I WANT TO FEEL

SOUL PROMPT ... I must

SCHEDULE ... reframe "obligations" into "choices"

- :
- :
- :
- :
- :
- :
- :
- :
- :
- :
- :
- :
- :
- :

3 THINGS ... that are moving your life forward

TO-DO ... prioritize pleasure

STOP DOING ... work for Love

WANT TO CHANGE ... the solution will come

GRATITUDE ... note WHY you're grateful

LOVE

Love how the light hits your life.

IDEAS. DESIRES. WISDOM. ... leave room for magic & meandering

When you assume your worth, you will value others more.

FIERCE

NOVEMBER

2017

communion

connected

connecting

connection

kind

kindness

devoted

devotion

friendship

home

integrity

love

loving

oneness

partnership

romantic

unity

whole

MONDAY	TUESDAY	WEDNESDAY
		All Saints' Day 1
WEEK 44		
6	7	8
WEEK 45		
13	14	15
WEEK 46		
20	Sun enters Sagittarius 21	22
WEEK 47		
27	28	29
WEEK 48		

THURSDAY	FRIDAY	SATURDAY	SUNDAY
All Souls' Day 2	3	○ Full Moon 4	**Daylight saving time ends** 5
9	10	**Veterans Day (US) Remembrance Day (CAN)** 11	12
16	17	● New Moon 18	19
Thanksgiving (US) 23	24	25	26
30			

NOVEMBER 2017 MONTHLY CHECK-IN

My Core Desired Feelings:

Feelings inform your wellness, your creations, your wisdom. Tune in to the predominant and new feelings that are running through you these days.

My major intentions & goals for the year:

Revisit your vision. When your core desired feelings lead the way, both your goals and how you go after them become more satisfying. How are your goals a reflection of how you most want to feel?

To generate my CDFs through my intentions & goals, I will:

What will it take to fulfill your vision for the year? Evaluate, affirm, or adjust your to-dos and intentions according to what you think will generate your core desired feelings along the way.

DIVINE CONNECTION

IDEAS. DESIRES. WISDOM. ... when you honour your time, you honour you

MYSTERIOUS

WHAT I WILL DO TO FEEL
THE WAY I WANT TO FEEL

SOUL PROMPT ... I will guard my

SCHEDULE ... does it light you up?

: ....
: ....
: ....
: ....
: ....
: ....
: ....
: ....
: ....
: ....
: ....
: ....
: ....
: ....

3 THINGS ... that are doable today

TO-DO ... less striving, more living

STOP DOING ... don't take any crap

WANT TO CHANGE ... clarity is power

GRATITUDE ... puts everything into perspective

TRUE
TANGIBLE

Defend your tenderness.

MY CORE DESIRED FEELINGS

WHAT I WILL DO TO FEEL
THE WAY I WANT TO FEEL

SOUL PROMPT ... today, my heart feels

SCHEDULE ... respect yourself

: ....

: ....

: ....

: ....

: ....

: ....

: ....

: ....

: ....

: ....

: ....

: ....

: ....

: ....

3 THINGS ... that matter most

....

....

TO-DO ... the WHOLE point is to feel good

....

....

....

....

....

STOP DOING ... does it feel light or heavy?

WANT TO CHANGE ... why should it be different?

GRATITUDE ... challenges are teachers

Call your power back.

SOUL-SATISFIED

WHAT I WILL DO TO FEEL
THE WAY I WANT TO FEEL

SOUL PROMPT ... I'm proud of

SCHEDULE ... joy expands time

:
:
:
:
:
:
:
:
:
:
:
:
:

3 THINGS ... because focus creates momentum

TO-DO ... it's your life. YOUR life. Your LIFE.

STOP DOING ... freedom is your birthright

WANT TO CHANGE ... naming it is liberating

GRATITUDE ... expands your consciousness

ENLIGHTENING

You are the centre of your universe.

SATURDAY November 4 | 2017
O Full Moon

SUNDAY November 5 | 2017
Daylight saving time ends

WHAT I WILL DO TO FEEL
THE WAY I WANT TO FEEL

TO-DO ... make choices that liberate you

TO-DO ... your desires are sacred

REFLECT ... this week I learned

ENVISION ... what do you *really* want to happen?

Consider the value of what you create for others.

RECOGNIZED

MY CORE DESIRED FEELINGS

WHAT I WILL DO TO FEEL
THE WAY I WANT TO FEEL

SOUL PROMPT ... if only I could

SCHEDULE ... simplicity is freedom

: ....
: ....
: ....
: ....
: ....
: ....
: ....
: ....
: ....
: ....
: ....
: ....
: ....
: ....

3 THINGS ... get this done and the rest is a bonus

....

....

....

TO-DO ... keep your soul on the agenda

....

....

....

....

....

STOP DOING ... *No* makes way for *Yes*

WANT TO CHANGE ... claim it. Tame it.

GRATITUDE ... specificity intensifies gratitude

We need each other to shine.

WHAT I WILL DO TO FEEL
THE WAY I WANT TO FEEL

SOUL PROMPT ... one word to describe my creative talent

SCHEDULE ... reframe "obligations" into "choices"

: ....
: ....
: ....
: ....
: ....
: ....
: ....
: ....
: ....
: ....
: ....
: ....
: ....

3 THINGS ... that are moving your life forward

TO-DO ... prioritize pleasure

STOP DOING ... work for Love

WANT TO CHANGE ... the solution will come

GRATITUDE ... note WHY you're grateful

Tell the truth and tell it fast.

FABULOUS

WHAT I WILL DO TO FEEL
THE WAY I WANT TO FEEL

SOUL PROMPT ... I learn best when

SCHEDULE ... does it light you up?

:

:

:

:

:

:

:

:

:

:

:

:

:

3 THINGS ... that are doable today

TO-DO ... less striving, more living

STOP DOING ... don't take any crap

WANT TO CHANGE ... clarity is power

GRATITUDE ... puts everything into perspective

IN COMMUNION

Shift the focus from "being loving" to "being Love itself".

MY CORE DESIRED FEELINGS

WHAT I WILL DO TO FEEL
THE WAY I WANT TO FEEL

SOUL PROMPT ... today, my heart feels

SCHEDULE ... respect yourself

:
:
:
:
:
:
:
:
:
:
:
:
:
:

3 THINGS ... that matter most

TO-DO ... the WHOLE point is to feel good

STOP DOING ... does it feel light or heavy?

WANT TO CHANGE ... why should it be different?

GRATITUDE ... challenges are teachers

Settling for crumbs doesn't keep you fed – it keeps you starving.

CENTRED

WHAT I WILL DO TO FEEL THE WAY I WANT TO FEEL

SOUL PROMPT ... who in your life right now do you really admire?

SCHEDULE ... joy expands time

- :
- :
- :
- :
- :
- :
- :
- :
- :
- :
- :
- :
- :

3 THINGS ... because focus creates momentum

TO-DO ... it's your life. YOUR life. Your LIFE.

STOP DOING ... freedom is your birthright

WANT TO CHANGE ... naming it is liberating

GRATITUDE ... expands your consciousness

SHINE

Question if you still Love what you once Loved.

WHAT I WILL DO TO FEEL
THE WAY I WANT TO FEEL

TO-DO ... make choices that liberate you

....

....

....

....

....

REFLECT ... ... what's true for you?

TO-DO ... your desires are sacred

....

....

....

....

....

ENVISION ... let it be easy

The job isn't done until you say "thank you".

FLAMBOYANT

MY CORE DESIRED FEELINGS

WHAT I WILL DO TO FEEL
THE WAY I WANT TO FEEL

SOUL PROMPT ... I have so much respect for

SCHEDULE ... simplicity is freedom

: ....

: ....

: ....

: ....

: ....

: ....

: ....

: ....

: ....

: ....

: ....

: ....

3 THINGS ... get this done and the rest is a bonus

....

....

....

TO-DO ... keep your soul on the agenda

....

....

....

....

....

STOP DOING ... *No* makes way for *Yes*

WANT TO CHANGE ... claim it. Tame it.

GRATITUDE ... specificity intensifies gratitude

DIVINELY INSPIRED

It's simple physics, really. More focused energy = more power.

TUESDAY November 14 | 2017

WHAT I WILL DO TO FEEL
THE WAY I WANT TO FEEL

SOUL PROMPT ... ecstatic Love

SCHEDULE ... reframe "obligations" into "choices"

- :
- :
- :
- :
- :
- :
- :
- :
- :
- :
- :
- :
- :
- :

3 THINGS ... that are moving your life forward

TO-DO ... prioritize pleasure

STOP DOING ... work for Love

WANT TO CHANGE ... the solution will come

GRATITUDE ... note WHY you're grateful

redefine what you think is possible

DAUNTLESS

WHAT I WILL DO TO FEEL
THE WAY I WANT TO FEEL

SOUL PROMPT ... best thing about my life right now is

SCHEDULE ... does it light you up?

3 THINGS ... that are doable today

TO-DO ... less striving, more living

STOP DOING ... don't take any crap

WANT TO CHANGE ... clarity is power

GRATITUDE ... puts everything into perspective

DISCIPLINED

Are you fixing your flaws, or exploring your potential?

MY CORE DESIRED FEELINGS

WHAT I WILL DO TO FEEL
THE WAY I WANT TO FEEL

SOUL PROMPT ... today, my heart feels

SCHEDULE ... respect yourself

:
:
:
:
:
:
:
:
:
:
:
:
:

3 THINGS ... that matter most

TO-DO ... the WHOLE point is to feel good

STOP DOING ... does it feel light or heavy?

WANT TO CHANGE ... why should it be different?

GRATITUDE ... challenges are teachers

You are changing.

EASE

MY CORE DESIRED FEELINGS

WHAT I WILL DO TO FEEL
THE WAY I WANT TO FEEL

SOUL PROMPT ... my greatest desire in relationships is

SCHEDULE ... joy expands time

- :
- :
- :
- :
- :
- :
- :
- :
- :
- :
- :
- :
- :

3 THINGS ... because focus creates momentum

TO-DO ... it's your life. YOUR life. Your LIFE.

STOP DOING ... freedom is your birthright

WANT TO CHANGE ... naming it is liberating

GRATITUDE ... expands your consciousness

ECSTATIC

It won't always be this way.

WHAT I WILL DO TO FEEL
THE WAY I WANT TO FEEL

TO-DO ... make choices that liberate you

TO-DO ... your desires are sacred

REFLECT ... speak up

ENVISION ... your soul is rooting for you

All hail the insatiable!

CELESTIAL

MY CORE DESIRED FEELINGS

WHAT I WILL DO TO FEEL
THE WAY I WANT TO FEEL

SOUL PROMPT ... I'm hot for

SCHEDULE ... simplicity is freedom

  :
  :
  :
  :
  :
  :
  :
  :
  :
  :
  :
  :
  :

3 THINGS ... get this done and the rest is a bonus

TO-DO ... keep your soul on the agenda

STOP DOING ... *No* makes way for *Yes*

WANT TO CHANGE ... claim it. Tame it.

GRATITUDE ... specificity intensifies gratitude

OF SERVICE

Serve the world with your joy.

MY CORE DESIRED FEELINGS

WHAT I WILL DO TO FEEL
THE WAY I WANT TO FEEL

SOUL PROMPT ... three other words for POWER

SCHEDULE ... reframe "obligations" into "choices"

:
:
:
:
:
:
:
:
:
:
:
:
:

3 THINGS ... that are moving your life forward

TO-DO ... prioritize pleasure

STOP DOING ... work for Love

WANT TO CHANGE ... the solution will come

GRATITUDE ... note WHY you're grateful

BRIGHT

Sometimes we forget to look at what we're holding on to. Take a look.

WHAT I WILL DO TO FEEL THE WAY I WANT TO FEEL

SOUL PROMPT ... I'm at peace with

SCHEDULE ... does it light you up?

3 THINGS ... that are doable today

TO-DO ... less striving, more living

STOP DOING ... don't take any crap

WANT TO CHANGE ... clarity is power

GRATITUDE ... puts everything into perspective

PROSPEROUS

Vividly envision how you want to feel.

MY CORE DESIRED FEELINGS

WHAT I WILL DO TO FEEL THE WAY I WANT TO FEEL

SOUL PROMPT ... today, my heart feels

SCHEDULE ... respect yourself

:
:
:
:
:
:
:
:
:
:
:
:
:
:

WANT TO CHANGE ... why should it be different?

3 THINGS ... that matter most

TO-DO ... the WHOLE point is to feel good

STOP DOING ... does it feel light or heavy?

GRATITUDE ... challenges are teachers

GROWING

Sometimes, the most enlightened thing to do is FIGHT BACK.

WHAT I WILL DO TO FEEL
THE WAY I WANT TO FEEL

SOUL PROMPT ... tomorrow will be

SCHEDULE ... joy expands time

3 THINGS ... because focus creates momentum

TO-DO ... it's your life. YOUR life. Your LIFE.

STOP DOING ... freedom is your birthright

WANT TO CHANGE ... naming it is liberating

GRATITUDE ... expands your consciousness

RADIANT

Negative feelings are wake-up calls.

WHAT I WILL DO TO FEEL
THE WAY I WANT TO FEEL

TO-DO ... make choices that liberate you

TO-DO ... your desires are sacred

REFLECT ... enthusiasm saves lives

ENVISION ... I'm devoted to

Sanction it with your Love.

POWERFUL

MY CORE DESIRED FEELINGS

WHAT I WILL DO TO FEEL THE WAY I WANT TO FEEL

SOUL PROMPT ... the easiest thing to do is

SCHEDULE ... simplicity is freedom

:
:
:
:
:
:
:
:
:
:
:
:
:

3 THINGS ... get this done and the rest is a bonus

TO-DO ... keep your soul on the agenda

STOP DOING ... *No* makes way for *Yes*

WANT TO CHANGE ... claim it. Tame it.

GRATITUDE ... specificity intensifies gratitude

RESTED

Clear desires = comfort in moments of pain.

MY CORE DESIRED FEELINGS

WHAT I WILL DO TO FEEL
THE WAY I WANT TO FEEL

SOUL PROMPT ... three words about my potential

SCHEDULE ... reframe "obligations" into "choices"

    :
    :
    :
    :
    :
    :
    :
    :
    :
    :
    :
    :
    :
    :

3 THINGS ... that are moving your life forward

TO-DO ... prioritize pleasure

STOP DOING ... work for Love

WANT TO CHANGE ... the solution will come

GRATITUDE ... note WHY you're grateful

Pressure creates diamonds.

UNTETHERED

WHAT I WILL DO TO FEEL
THE WAY I WANT TO FEEL

SOUL PROMPT ... I'm feeling tender about

SCHEDULE ... does it light you up?

: ....
: ....
: ....
: ....
: ....
: ....
: ....
: ....
: ....
: ....
: ....
: ....
: ....

3 THINGS ... that are doable today

....
....
....

TO-DO ... less striving, more living

....
....
....
....
....

STOP DOING ... don't take any crap

WANT TO CHANGE ... clarity is power

GRATITUDE ... puts everything into perspective

RESPLENDENT

Don't privilege overly needy types.

MY CORE DESIRED FEELINGS

WHAT I WILL DO TO FEEL
THE WAY I WANT TO FEEL

SOUL PROMPT ... when I feel loving, I

SCHEDULE ... respect yourself

3 THINGS ... that matter most

:
:
:
:

TO-DO ... the WHOLE point is to feel good

:
:
:
:
:
:
:

STOP DOING ... does it feel light or heavy?

:
:
:

WANT TO CHANGE ... why should it be different?

GRATITUDE ... challenges are teachers

Speak clearly about your past.

ZEN

DECEMBER

DECEMBER

authentic

bright

brightened

brilliance

brilliant

enlightened

genuine

gold

golden

illuminated

light

lightness

lit up

luminous

spirit

spiritual

wonder

wondrous

MONDAY	TUESDAY	WEDNESDAY
WEEK 48		
4	5	6
WEEK 49		
11	**Hanukkah begins (evening)** 12	13
WEEK 50		
● New Moon 18	19	**Hanukkah ends (evening)** 20
WEEK 51		
Christmas Day 25	**Kwanzaa begins Boxing Day** 26	27
WEEK 52		

THURSDAY	FRIDAY	SATURDAY	SUNDAY
	1	2	**First Sunday of Advent** 3 O Full Moon Mercury goes retrograde
7	8	9	10
14	15	16	17
Winter Solstice/ Yule 21 Sun enters Capricorn	Mercury turns direct 22	23	**Christmas Eve** 24
28	29	30	**New Year's Eve** 31

DECEMBER 2017 MONTHLY CHECK-IN

My Core Desired Feelings:

Feelings inform your wellness, your creations, your wisdom. Tune in to the predominant and new feelings that are running through you these days.

My major intentions & goals for the year:

Revisit your vision. When your core desired feelings lead the way, both your goals and how you go after them become more satisfying. How are your goals a reflection of how you most want to feel?

To generate my CDFs through my intentions & goals, I will:

What will it take to fulfill your vision for the year? Evaluate, affirm, or adjust your to-dos and intentions according to what you think will generate your core desired feelings along the way.

OPENNESS

IDEAS. DESIRES. WISDOM. ... feel free

INTENTIONAL

MY CORE DESIRED FEELINGS

WHAT I WILL DO TO FEEL THE WAY I WANT TO FEEL

SOUL PROMPT ... my bedtime ritual

SCHEDULE ... joy expands time

:
:
:
:
:
:
:
:
:
:
:
:
:
:

3 THINGS ... because focus creates momentum

TO-DO ... it's your life. YOUR life. Your LIFE.

STOP DOING ... freedom is your birthright

WANT TO CHANGE ... naming it is liberating

GRATITUDE ... expands your consciousness

WHOOSH

Prioritizing good sleep is good self Love.

SATURDAY December 2 | 2017

SUNDAY December 3 | 2017

First Sunday of Advent
O Full Moon | Mercury goes retrograde

WHAT I WILL DO TO FEEL
THE WAY I WANT TO FEEL

TO-DO ... make choices that liberate you

TO-DO ... your desires are sacred

REFLECT ... rest

ENVISION ... don't hold back

Fire your inner critic.

GENUINE

WHAT I WILL DO TO FEEL
THE WAY I WANT TO FEEL

SOUL PROMPT ... I worship

SCHEDULE ... simplicity is freedom

:
:
:
:
:
:
:
:
:
:
:
:
:

WANT TO CHANGE ... claim it. Tame it.

3 THINGS ... get this done and the rest is a bonus

TO-DO ... keep your soul on the agenda

STOP DOING ... *No* makes way for *Yes*

GRATITUDE ... specificity intensifies gratitude

BRIGHT JOY

When the phoenix rises from the flames, she is even more beautiful than before.

MY CORE DESIRED FEELINGS

WHAT I WILL DO TO FEEL
THE WAY I WANT TO FEEL

SOUL PROMPT ... I feel so blessed to

SCHEDULE ... reframe "obligations" into "choices"

:
:
:
:
:
:
:
:
:
:
:
:
:

3 THINGS ... that are moving your life forward

TO-DO ... prioritize pleasure

STOP DOING ... work for Love

WANT TO CHANGE ... the solution will come

GRATITUDE ... note WHY you're grateful

Choose to shine.

EVER-
EXPANDING

WHAT I WILL DO TO FEEL
THE WAY I WANT TO FEEL

SOUL PROMPT ... I surrender to

SCHEDULE ... does it light you up?

- :
- :
- :
- :
- :
- :
- :
- :
- :
- :
- :
- :
- :

3 THINGS ... that are doable today

TO-DO ... less striving, more living

STOP DOING ... don't take any crap

WANT TO CHANGE ... clarity is power

GRATITUDE ... puts everything into perspective

DEDICATED

I'm not grateful for all of it. But I'm grateful for what I learned from it.

WHAT I WILL DO TO FEEL
THE WAY I WANT TO FEEL

SOUL PROMPT ... today, my heart feels

SCHEDULE ... respect yourself

3 THINGS ... that matter most

:
:
:
:

TO-DO ... the WHOLE point is to feel good

:
:
:
:
:

STOP DOING ... does it feel light or heavy?

:
:
:

WANT TO CHANGE ... why should it be different?

GRATITUDE ... challenges are teachers

Manifestation requires clear intention.

BRILLIANT

WHAT I WILL DO TO FEEL
THE WAY I WANT TO FEEL

SOUL PROMPT ... who will you thank today?

SCHEDULE ... joy expands time

- :
- :
- :
- :
- :
- :
- :
- :
- :
- :
- :
- :
- :
- :

3 THINGS ... because focus creates momentum

TO-DO ... it's your life. YOUR life. Your LIFE.

STOP DOING ... freedom is your birthright

WANT TO CHANGE ... naming it is liberating

GRATITUDE ... expands your consciousness

GRATEFUL

You don't need their approval.

WHAT I WILL DO TO   FEEL
THE WAY I WANT TO FEEL

TO-DO ... make choices that liberate you

TO-DO ... your desires are sacred

REFLECT ... this week I learned

ENVISION ... what do you *really* want to happen?

Choose the joy.

DARING

MY CORE DESIRED FEELINGS

WHAT I WILL DO TO FEEL
THE WAY I WANT TO FEEL

SOUL PROMPT ... I'm done with

SCHEDULE ... simplicity is freedom

: ....

: ....

: ....

: ....

: ....

: ....

: ....

: ....

: ....

: ....

: ....

: ....

: ....

: ....

3 THINGS ... get this done and the rest is a bonus

....

....

TO-DO ... keep your soul on the agenda

....

....

....

....

....

STOP DOING ... *No* makes way for *Yes*

WANT TO CHANGE ... claim it. Tame it.

GRATITUDE ... specificity intensifies gratitude

ABUNDANCE

Avoiding conclusions can be a monumental act of Love.

MY CORE DESIRED FEELINGS

WHAT I WILL DO TO FEEL
THE WAY I WANT TO FEEL

SOUL PROMPT ... I'm very aware of

SCHEDULE ... reframe "obligations" into "choices"

- :
- :
- :
- :
- :
- :
- :
- :
- :
- :
- :
- :
- :
- :

3 THINGS ... that are moving your life forward

TO-DO ... prioritize pleasure

STOP DOING ... work for Love

WANT TO CHANGE ... the solution will come

GRATITUDE ... note WHY you're grateful

Raise your standards and the universe will meet you there.

DIVINE

WHAT I WILL DO TO FEEL
THE WAY I WANT TO FEEL

SOUL PROMPT ... I don't regret

SCHEDULE ... does it light you up?

: ....
: ....
: ....
: ....
: ....
: ....
: ....
: ....
: ....
: ....
: ....
: ....
: ....

3 THINGS ... that are doable today

....
....
....

TO-DO ... less striving, more living

....
....
....
....

STOP DOING ... don't take any crap

WANT TO CHANGE ... clarity is power

GRATITUDE ... puts everything into perspective

SOLACE

Your definition of what's sacred will change over time.

MY CORE DESIRED FEELINGS

WHAT I WILL DO TO FEEL THE WAY I WANT TO FEEL

SOUL PROMPT ... today, my heart feels

SCHEDULE ... respect yourself

:
:
:
:
:
:
:
:
:
:
:
:
:
:

3 THINGS ... that matter most

TO-DO ... the WHOLE point is to feel good

STOP DOING ... does it feel light or heavy?

WANT TO CHANGE ... why should it be different?

GRATITUDE ... challenges are teachers

Destroy before you create. So scary. So effective.

INSTINCTIVE

MY CORE DESIRED FEELINGS

WHAT I WILL DO TO FEEL THE WAY I WANT TO FEEL

SOUL PROMPT ... integrity is

SCHEDULE ... joy expands time

- :
- :
- :
- :
- :
- :
- :
- :
- :
- :
- :
- :
- :

3 THINGS ... because focus creates momentum

TO-DO ... it's your life. YOUR life. Your LIFE.

STOP DOING ... freedom is your birthright

WANT TO CHANGE ... naming it is liberating

GRATITUDE ... expands your consciousness

PURPOSEFUL

Angels are waiting for your call.

WHAT I WILL DO TO FEEL
THE WAY I WANT TO FEEL

TO-DO ... make choices that liberate you

TO-DO ... your desires are sacred

REFLECT ... what's true for you?

ENVISION ... let it be easy

Half truths piled on top of half truths do not add up to the whole truth.

SIGNIFICANT

MY CORE DESIRED FEELINGS

WHAT I WILL DO TO FEEL THE WAY I WANT TO FEEL

SOUL PROMPT ... I adore

SCHEDULE ... simplicity is freedom

- :
- :
- :
- :
- :
- :
- :
- :
- :
- :
- :
- :
- :

3 THINGS ... get this done and the rest is a bonus

TO-DO ... keep your soul on the agenda

STOP DOING ... *No* makes way for *Yes*

WANT TO CHANGE ... claim it. Tame it.

GRATITUDE ... specificity intensifies gratitude

TRUST

It's all medicine.

WHAT I WILL DO TO FEEL THE WAY I WANT TO FEEL

SOUL PROMPT ... I treasure

SCHEDULE ... reframe "obligations" into "choices"

:
:
:
:
:
:
:
:
:
:
:
:
:

3 THINGS ... that are moving your life forward

TO-DO ... prioritize pleasure

STOP DOING ... work for Love

WANT TO CHANGE ... the solution will come

GRATITUDE ... note WHY you're grateful

The future you desire deserves your full attention.

PRESENT

MY CORE DESIRED FEELINGS

WHAT I WILL DO TO FEEL
THE WAY I WANT TO FEEL

SOUL PROMPT ... my superpower is

SCHEDULE ... does it light you up?

3 THINGS ... that are doable today

TO-DO ... less striving, more living

STOP DOING ... don't take any crap

WANT TO CHANGE ... clarity is power

GRATITUDE ... puts everything into perspective

SOVEREIGN

Suspend judgment as a practice of faith.

THURSDAY December 21 | 2017

Winter Solstice/Yule
Sun enters Capricorn

MY CORE DESIRED FEELINGS

WHAT I WILL DO TO FEEL
THE WAY I WANT TO FEEL

SOUL PROMPT ... today, my heart feels

SCHEDULE ... respect yourself

3 THINGS ... that matter most

TO-DO ... the WHOLE point is to feel good

STOP DOING ... does it feel light or heavy?

WANT TO CHANGE ... why should it be different?

GRATITUDE ... challenges are teachers

Make a new vow.

VIVID

MY CORE DESIRED FEELINGS

WHAT I WILL DO TO FEEL
THE WAY I WANT TO FEEL

SOUL PROMPT ... my faith in . . . . is strong.

SCHEDULE ... joy expands time

3 THINGS ... because focus creates momentum

:
:
:
:

TO-DO ... it's your life. YOUR life. Your LIFE.

:
:
:
:
:
:
:

STOP DOING ... freedom is your birthright

:
:
:

WANT TO CHANGE ... naming it is liberating

GRATITUDE ... expands your consciousness

CREATIVE

respect all the work you've done

WHAT I WILL DO TO FEEL
THE WAY I WANT TO FEEL

TO-DO ... make choices that liberate you

TO-DO ... your desires are sacred

REFLECT ... speak up

ENVISION ... your soul is rooting for you

Love things just the way they are and watch what happens.

CURIOUS

WHAT I WILL DO TO FEEL THE WAY I WANT TO FEEL

SOUL PROMPT ... I am celebrating

SCHEDULE ... simplicity is freedom

:

:

:

:

:

:

:

:

:

:

:

:

:

:

3 THINGS ... get this done and the rest is a bonus

TO-DO ... keep your soul on the agenda

STOP DOING ... *No* makes way for *Yes*

WANT TO CHANGE ... claim it. Tame it.

GRATITUDE ... specificity intensifies gratitude

ENDURING

Your heart is a light source.

TUESDAY December 26 | 2017
Kwanzaa begins | Boxing Day

MY CORE DESIRED FEELINGS

WHAT I WILL DO TO FEEL
THE WAY I WANT TO FEEL

SOUL PROMPT ... I wonder about

SCHEDULE ... reframe "obligations" into "choices"

:
:
:
:
:
:
:
:
:
:
:
:
:
:

3 THINGS ... that are moving your life forward

TO-DO ... prioritize pleasure

STOP DOING ... work for Love

WANT TO CHANGE ... the solution will come

GRATITUDE ... note WHY you're grateful

Receive the Love that is being offered.

BOLD

WHAT I WILL DO TO FEEL
THE WAY I WANT TO FEEL

SOUL PROMPT ... I choose

SCHEDULE ... does it light you up?

:
:
:
:
:
:
:
:
:
:
:
:
:

3 THINGS ... that are doable today

TO-DO ... less striving, more living

STOP DOING ... don't take any crap

WANT TO CHANGE ... clarity is power

GRATITUDE ... puts everything into perspective

FIRECRACKER

Wanting more for your future is not a betrayal of your past.

MY CORE DESIRED FEELINGS

WHAT I WILL DO TO FEEL
THE WAY I WANT TO FEEL

SOUL PROMPT ... today, my heart feels

SCHEDULE ... respect yourself

: ⋯
: ⋯
: ⋯
: ⋯
: ⋯
: ⋯
: ⋯
: ⋯
: ⋯
: ⋯
: ⋯
: ⋯
: ⋯
: ⋯

3 THINGS ... that matter most

TO-DO ... the WHOLE point is to feel good

STOP DOING ... does it feel light or heavy?

WANT TO CHANGE ... why should it be different?

GRATITUDE ... challenges are teachers

It won't be long now.

DEEPLY LOVED

MY CORE DESIRED FEELINGS

WHAT I WILL DO TO FEEL
THE WAY I WANT TO FEEL

SOUL PROMPT ... I bless

SCHEDULE ... joy expands time

:
:
:
:
:
:
:
:
:
:
:
:
:

3 THINGS ... because focus creates momentum

TO-DO ... it's your life. YOUR life. Your LIFE.

STOP DOING ... freedom is your birthright

WANT TO CHANGE ... naming it is liberating

GRATITUDE ... expands your consciousness

PROGRESSIVE

Shatter the legacy that's holding you back.

WHAT I WILL DO TO FEEL
THE WAY I WANT TO FEEL

TO-DO ... make choices that liberate you

TO-DO ... your desires are sacred

REFLECT ... enthusiasm saves lives

ENVISION ... I'm devoted to

Everything is about to change.

FORGIVING

Compassion is so often the solution